Gardens of Sapporo, Japan

A TRAVEL PHOTO ART BOOK

LAINE CUNNINGHAM

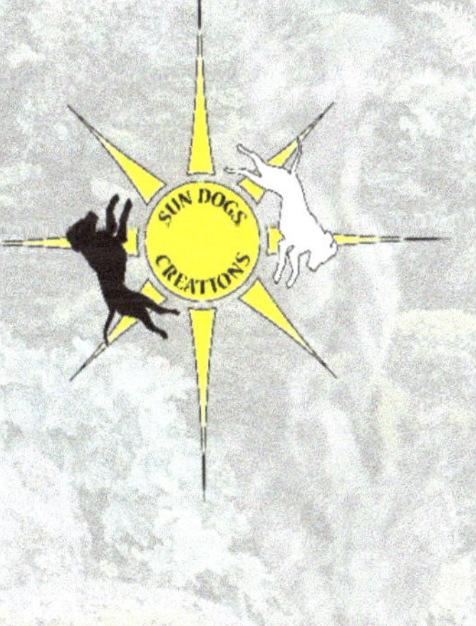

Gardens of Sapporo, Japan

A Travel Photo Art Book

Published by Sun Dogs Creations
Changing the World One Book at a Time
Print ISBN: 978-1-951389-32-1

Cover Image by Laine Cunningham
Cover Design by Angel Leya

While Sapporo, Japan boasts a number of formal botanical sites, visitors delight in the meditative beauty found in public flower beds and private front gardens. Common flowering varieties include chrysanthemum and, if the space boasts a water feature, water iris. Hydrangeas hug walls while azaleas fill the spaces beneath red and white pines.

As Japan's northernmost city, Sapporo covers more area than any other city in the country. Still, the amount of space available for gardening is small. Residents make the best use of tiny plots in front of their homes, behind apartment buildings, and along the strips between sidewalks and streets. Containers extend the gardens up steps and onto patios.

These beautiful plots are as unique as the people who plant and tend them. Many utilize local stones to mimic the rise of mountains. Pines are cloud pruned, a labor-intensive process that results in a tidy, uplifting shape. Wood elements, whether decorative or functional, are left untreated so as to weather naturally. Although the blooms in these gardens can be spectacular, the Japanese approach values the sculptural shape of plants and the garden's layout over a profusion of blossoms.

Stroll through the private and public garden spaces presented in *Gardens of Sapporo, Japan* to appreciate a meditative aesthetic.

CORKSCREW

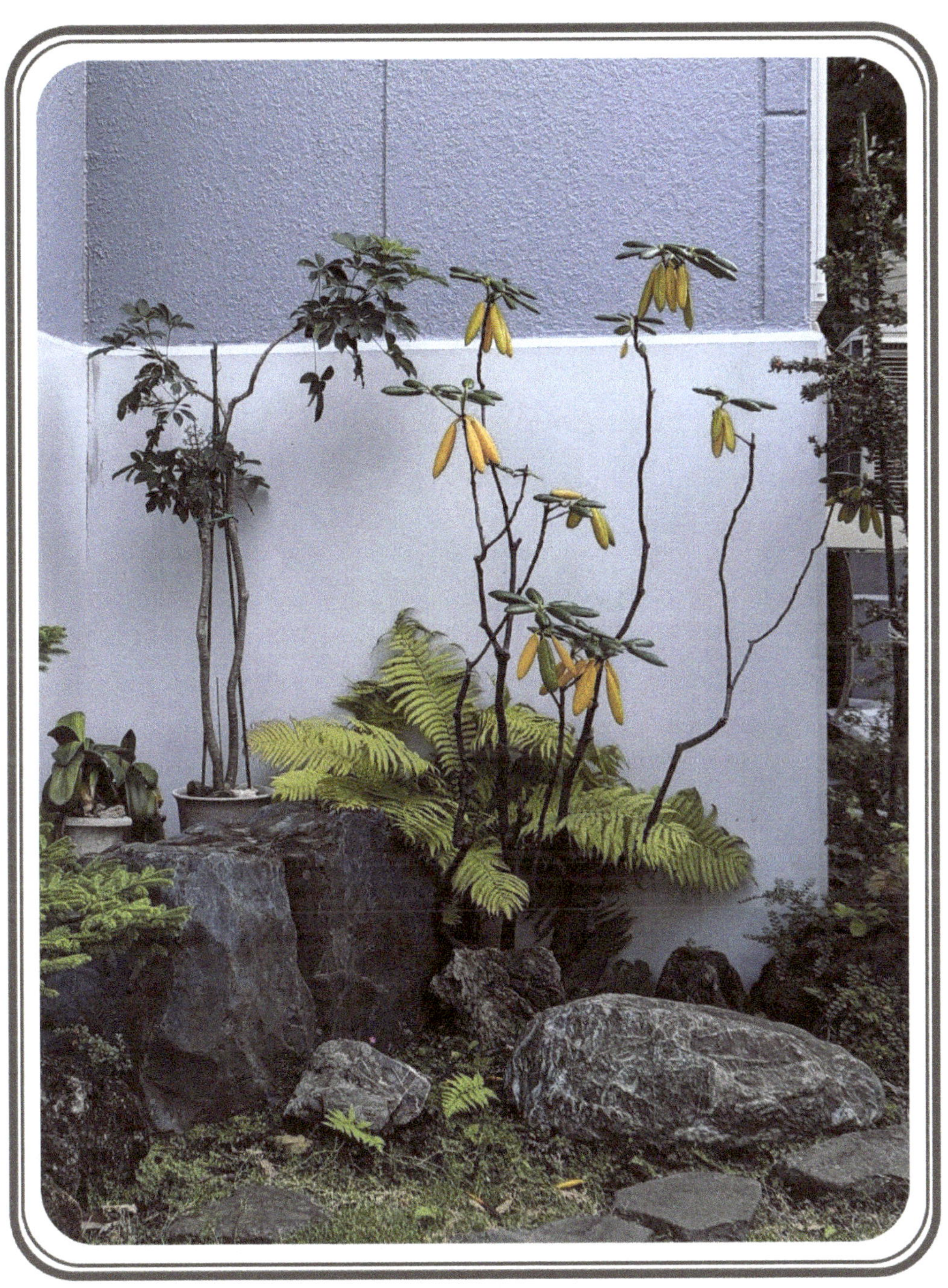

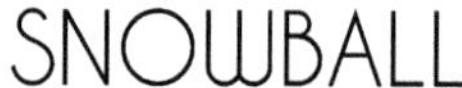
SNOWBALL

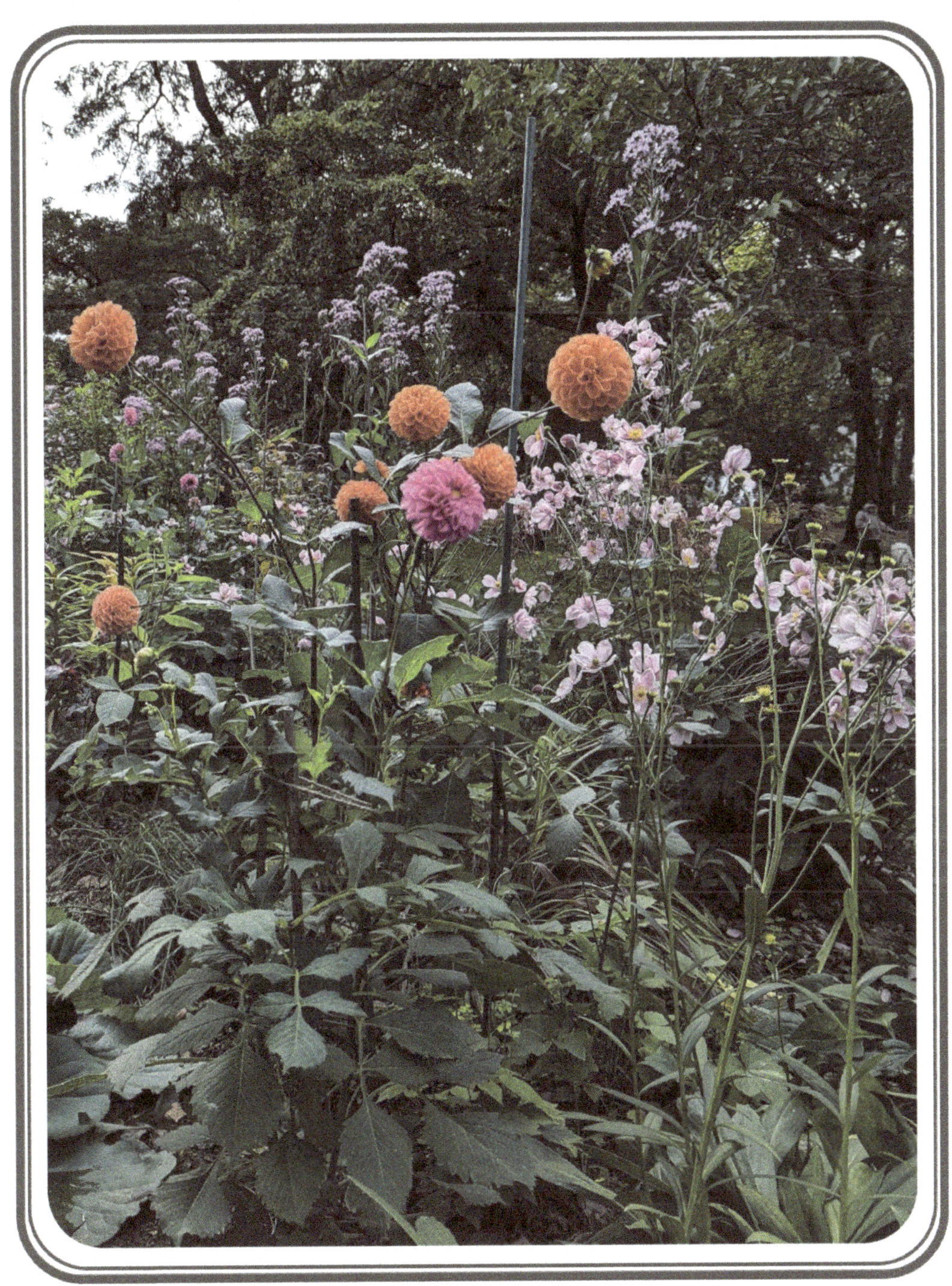

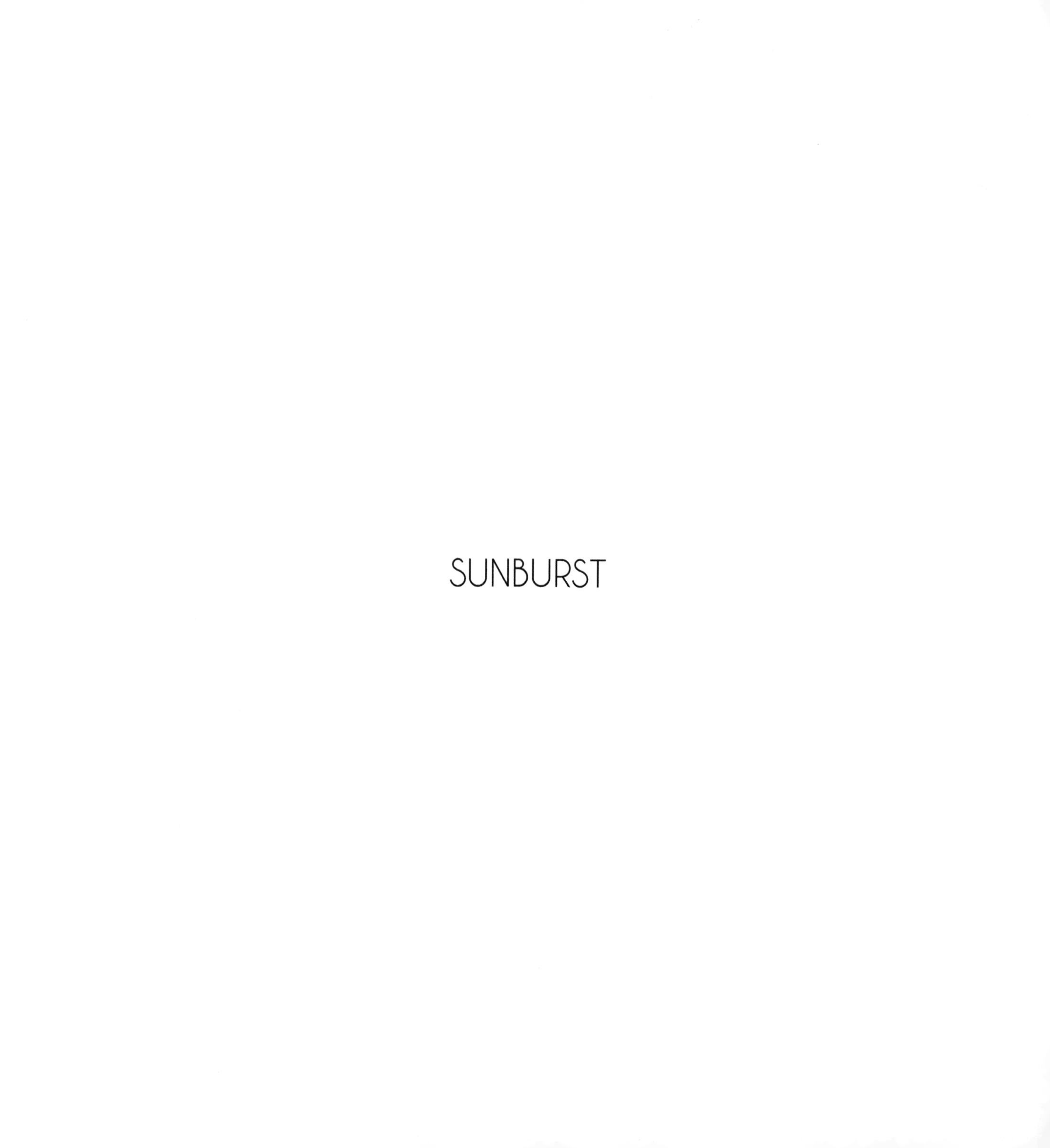

SUNBURST

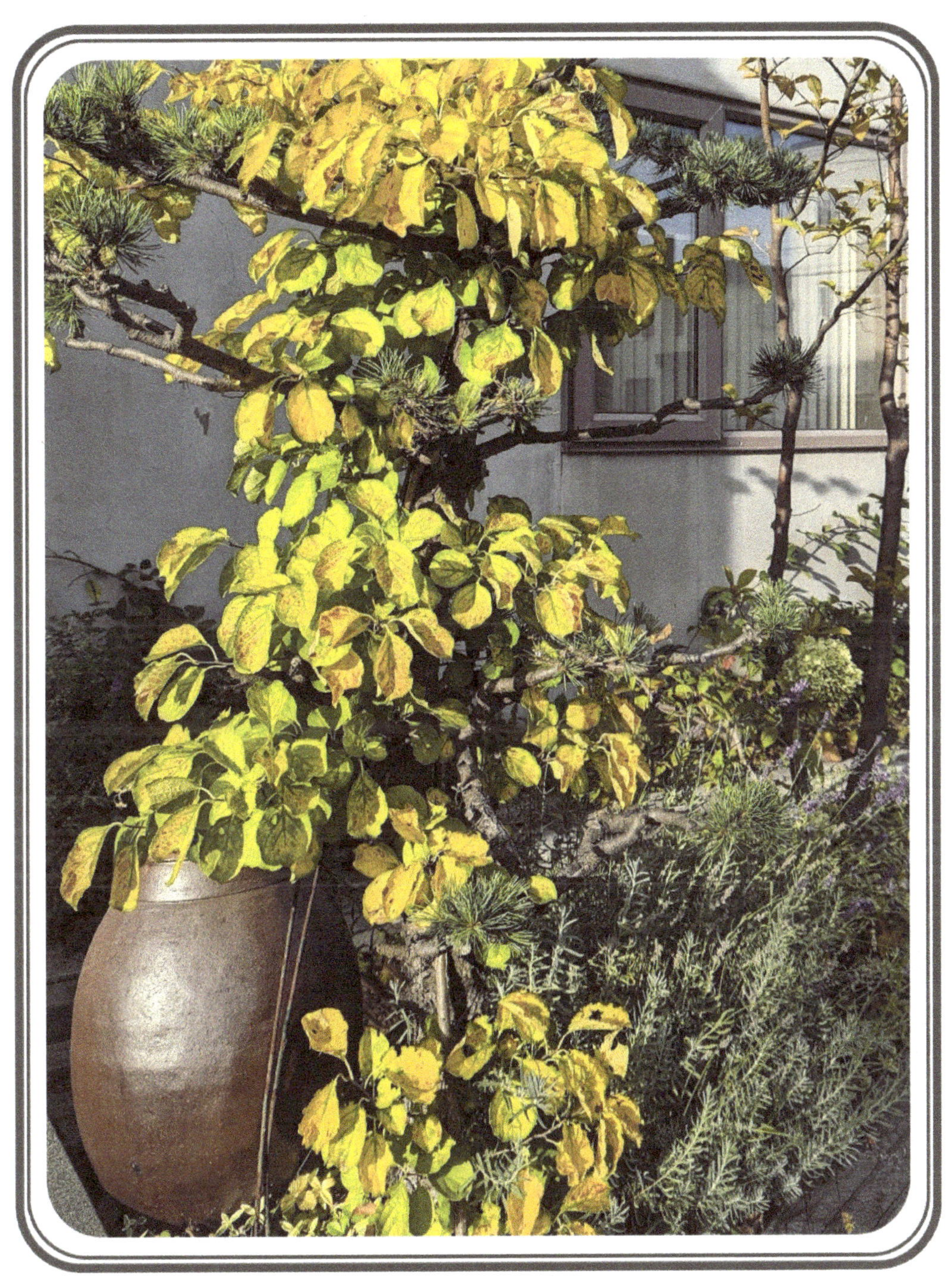

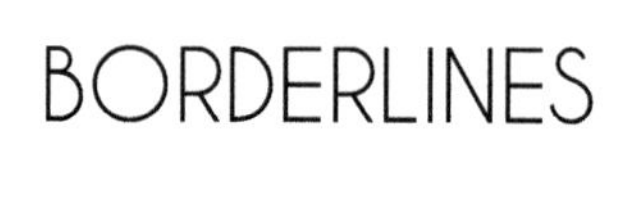
BORDERLINES

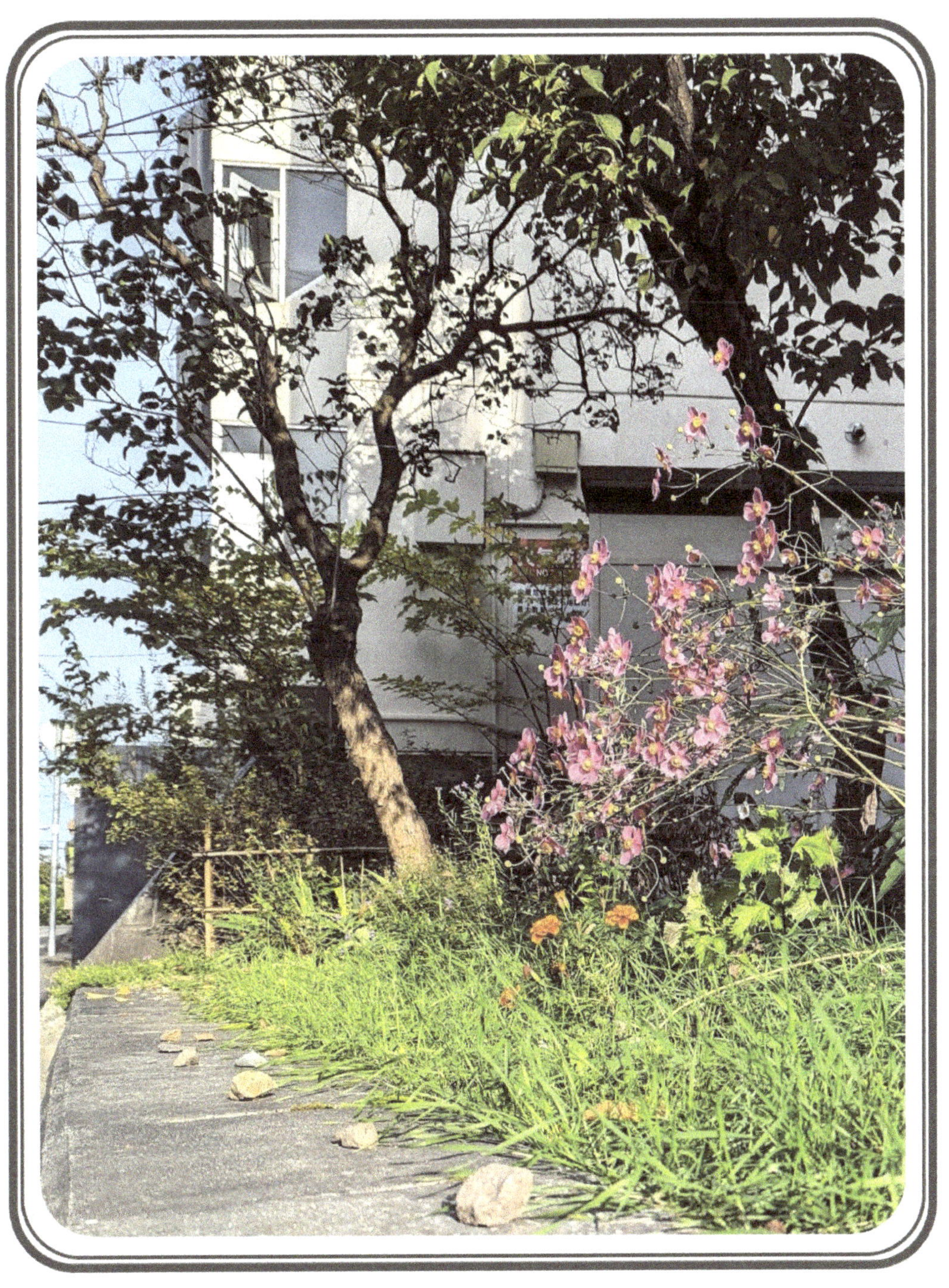

LIMBER

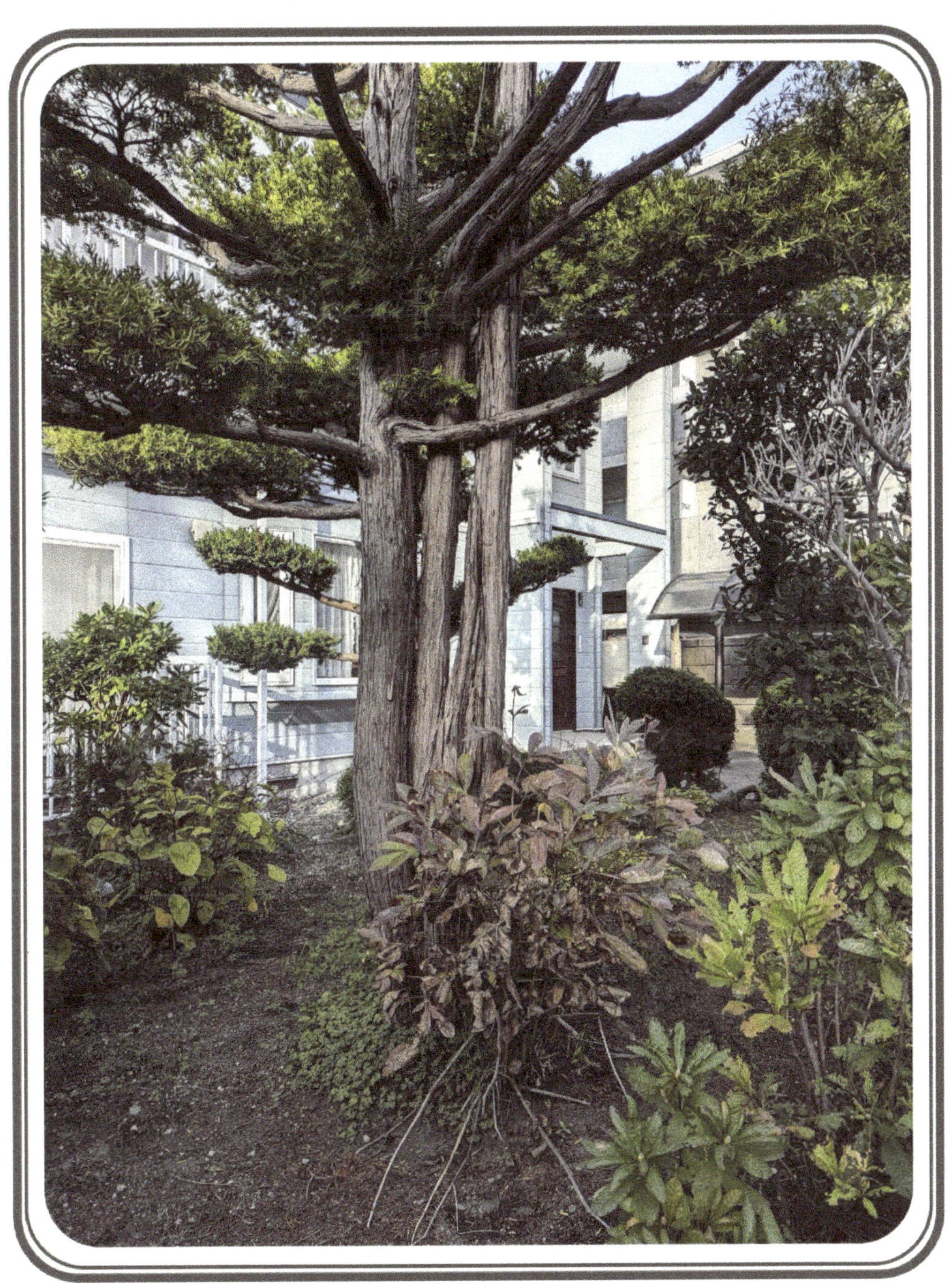

HELIX

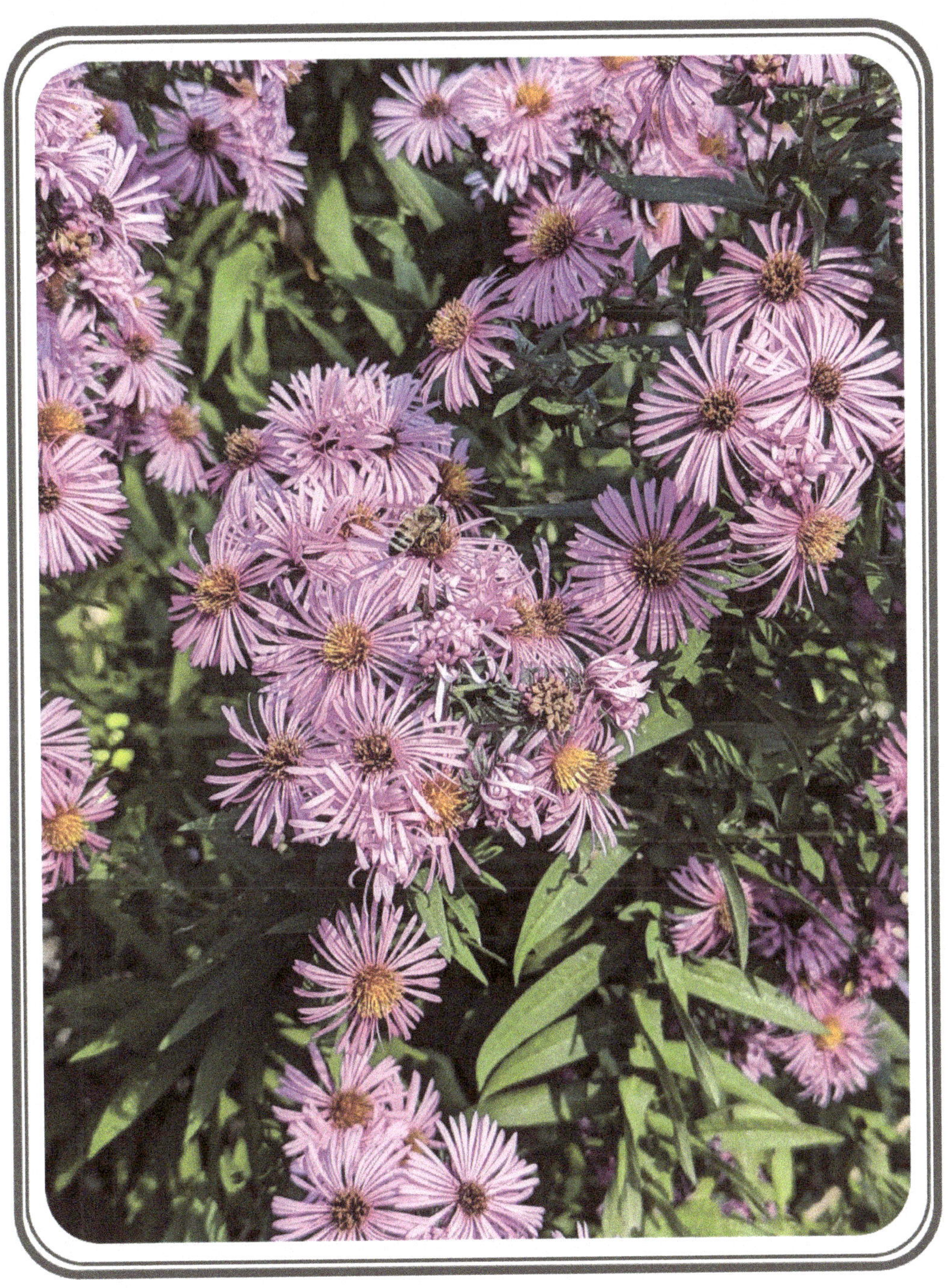

PUFF

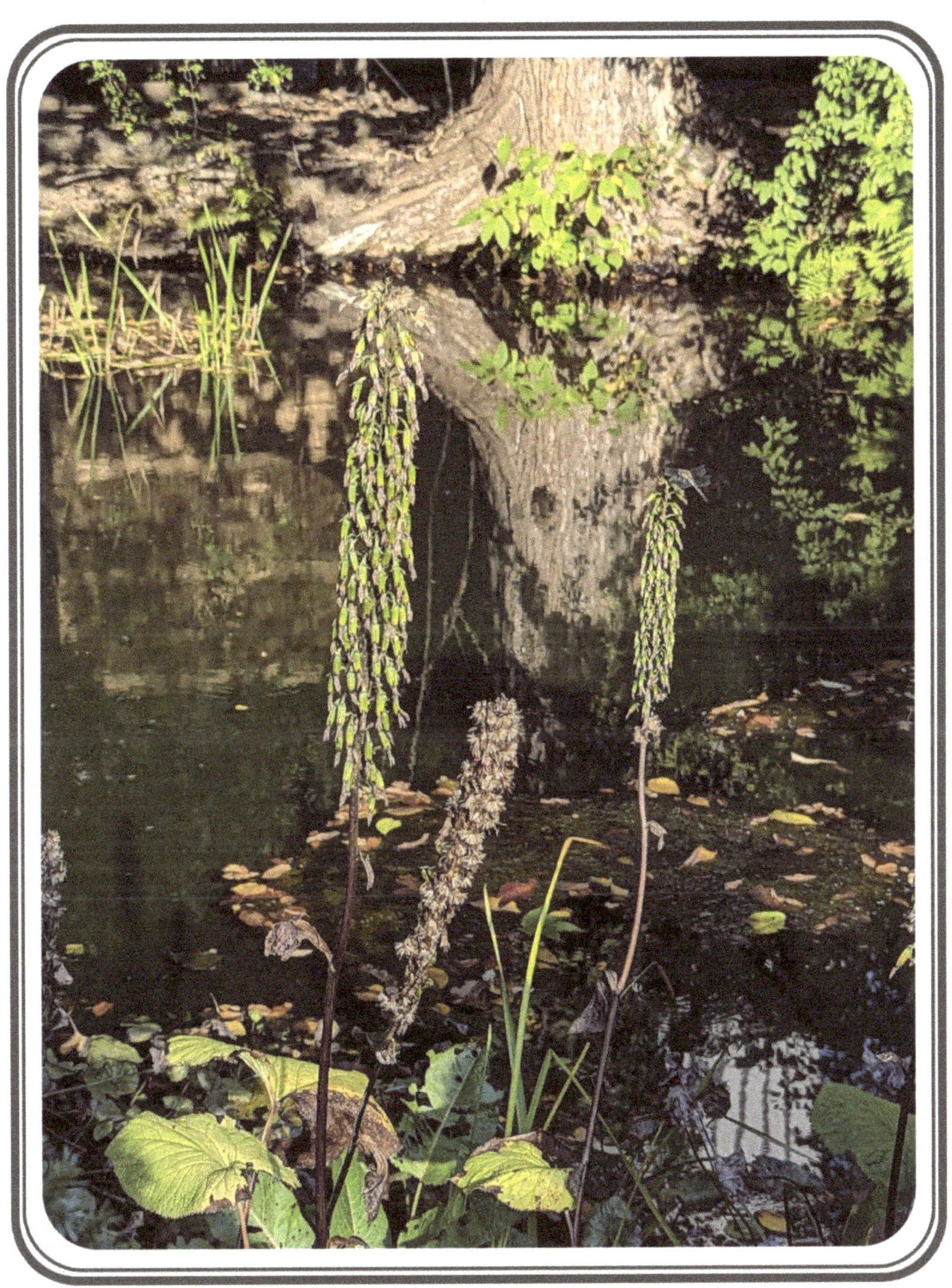

BACKDROP

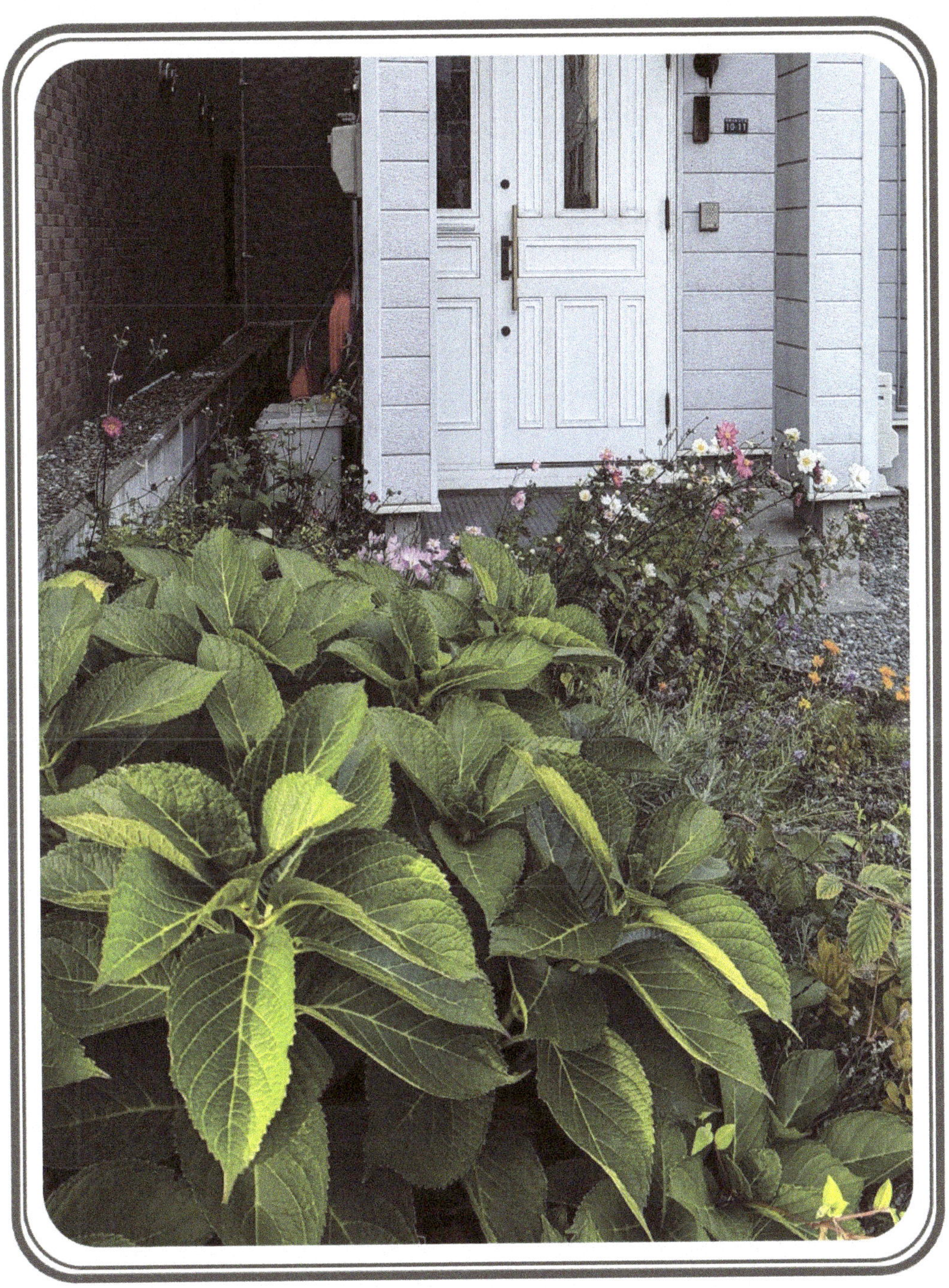

OBTUSE

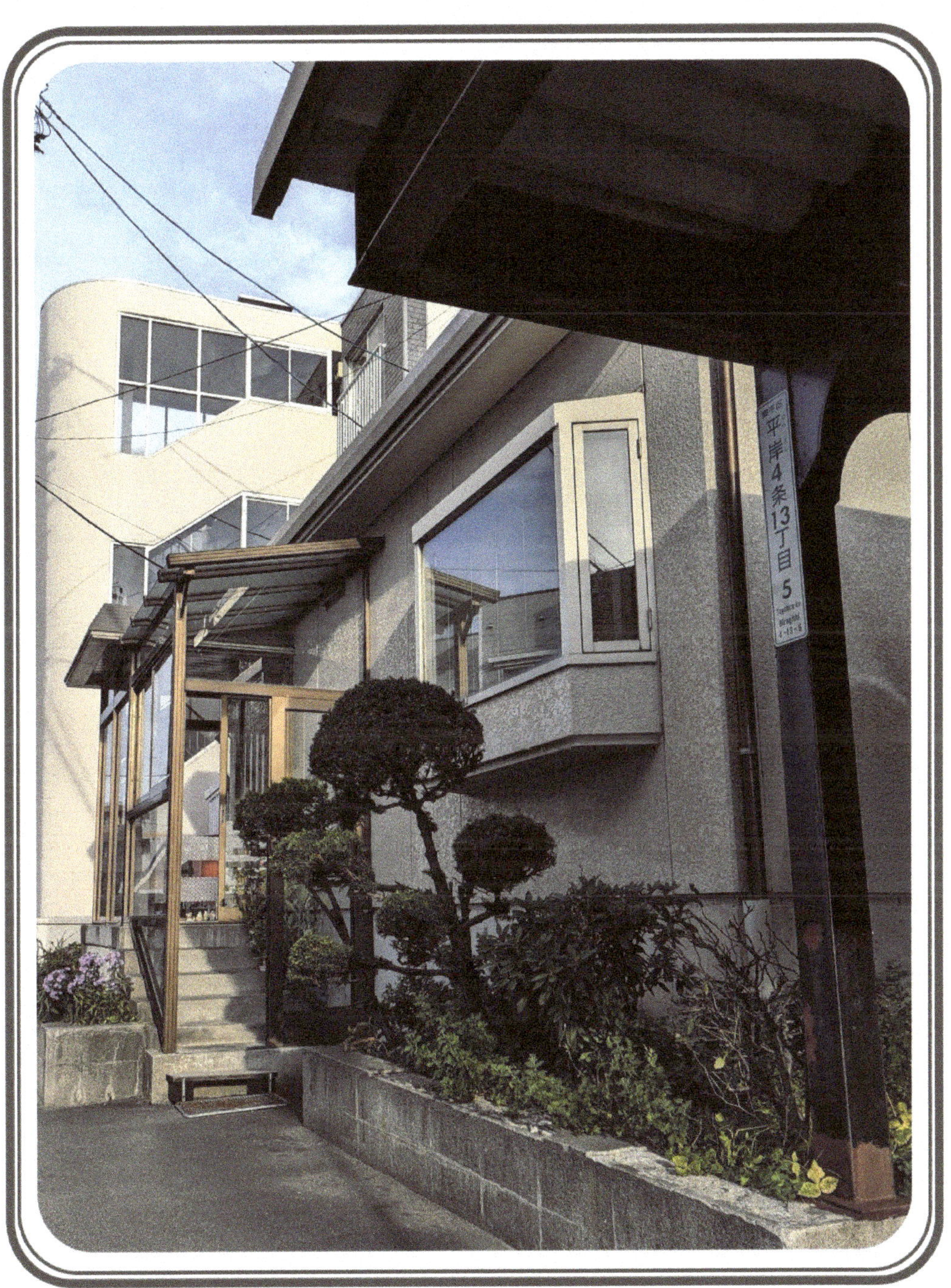
平岸4条13丁目
5

DELIGHT

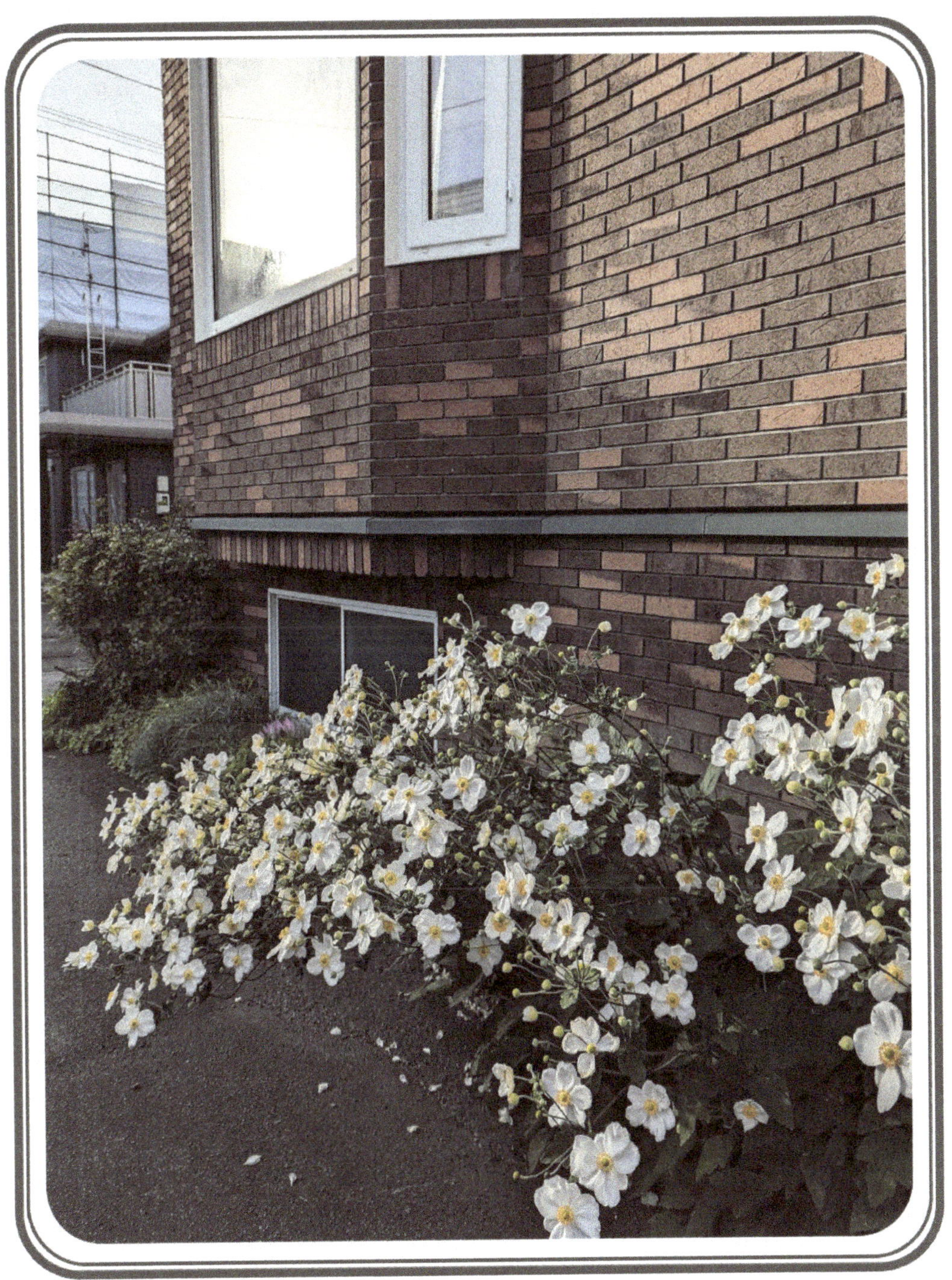

FELICITY

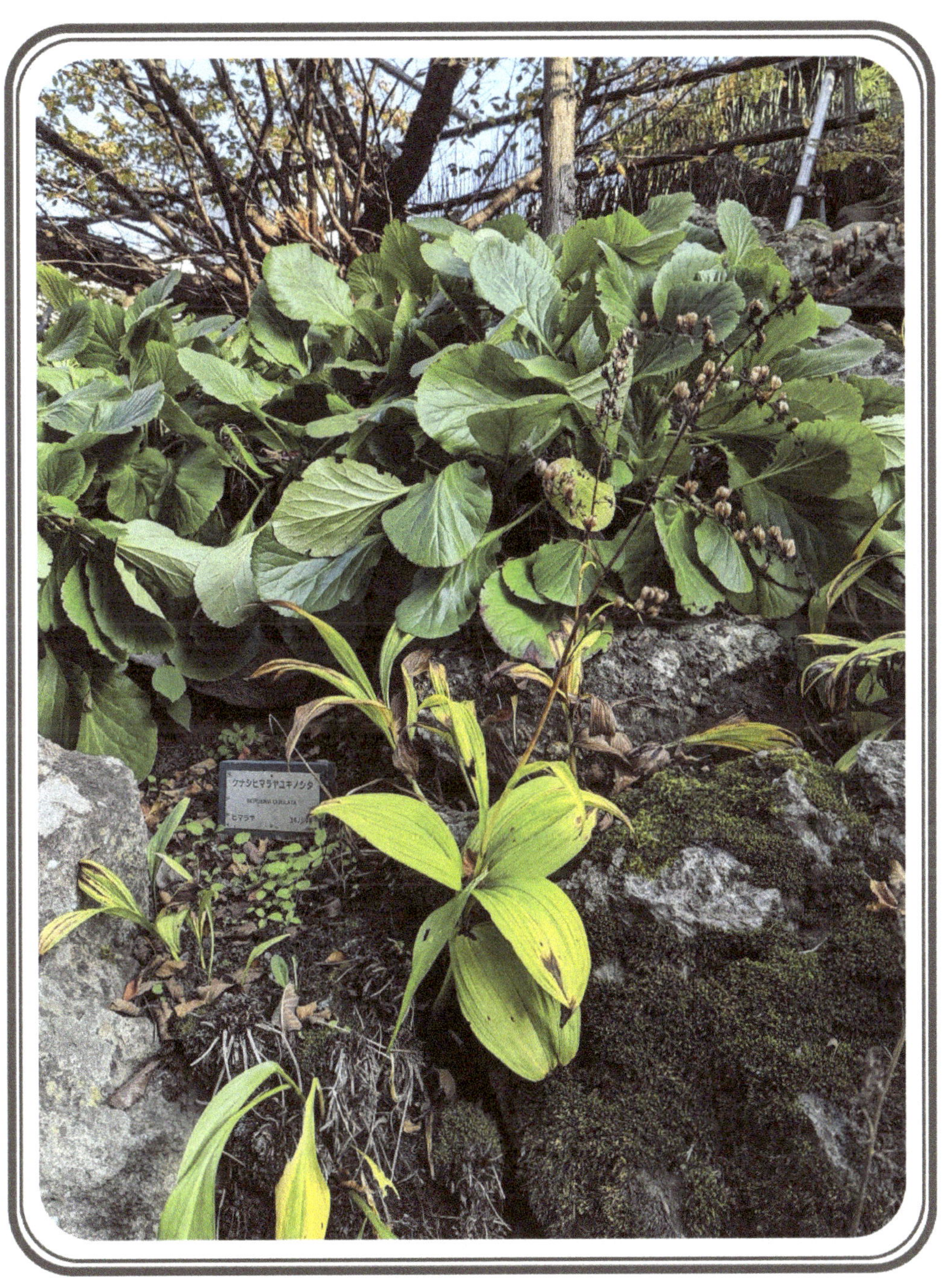
クナシヒマラヤユキノシタ
ヒマラヤ

RUNWAY

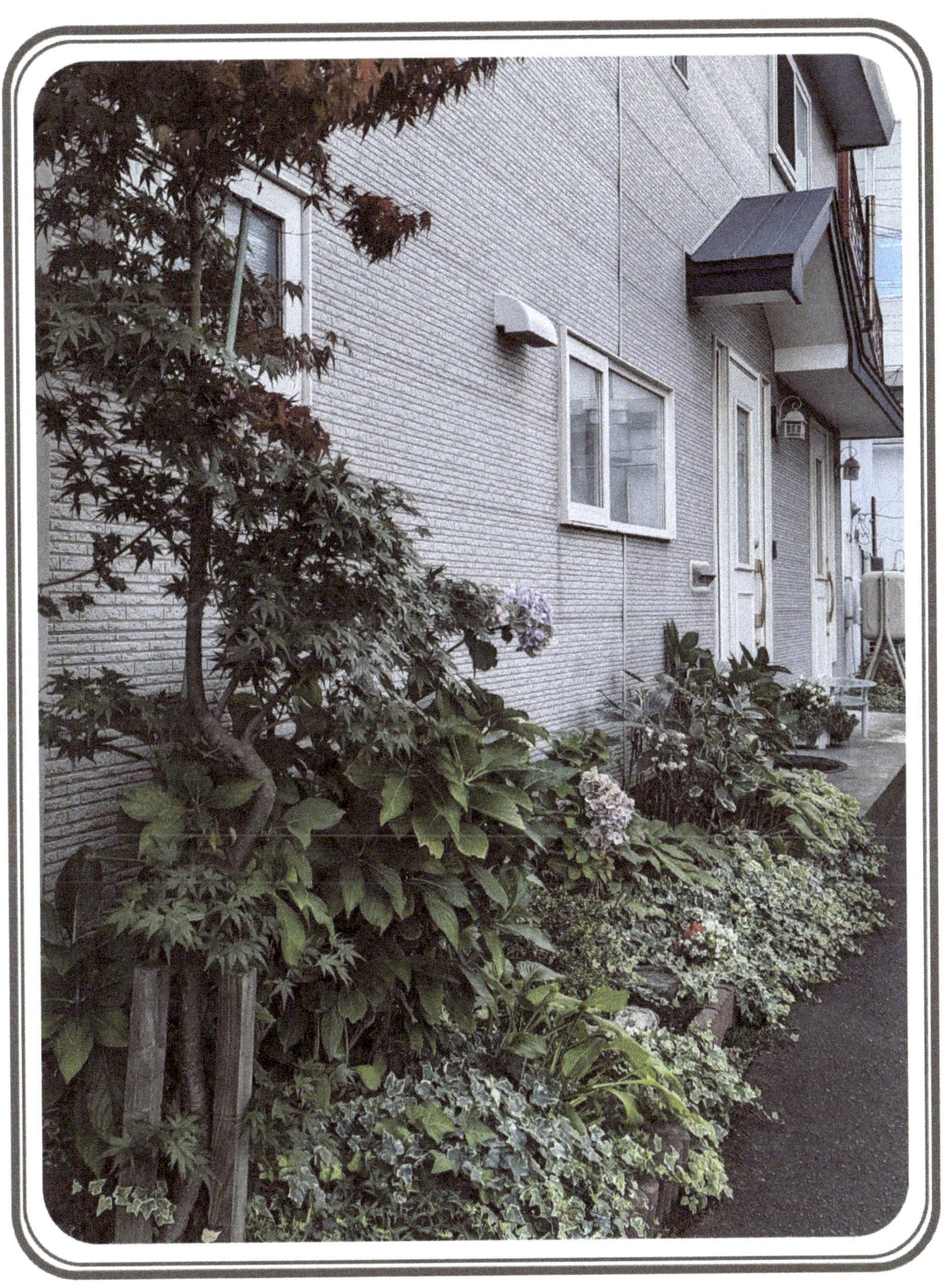

POPCORN

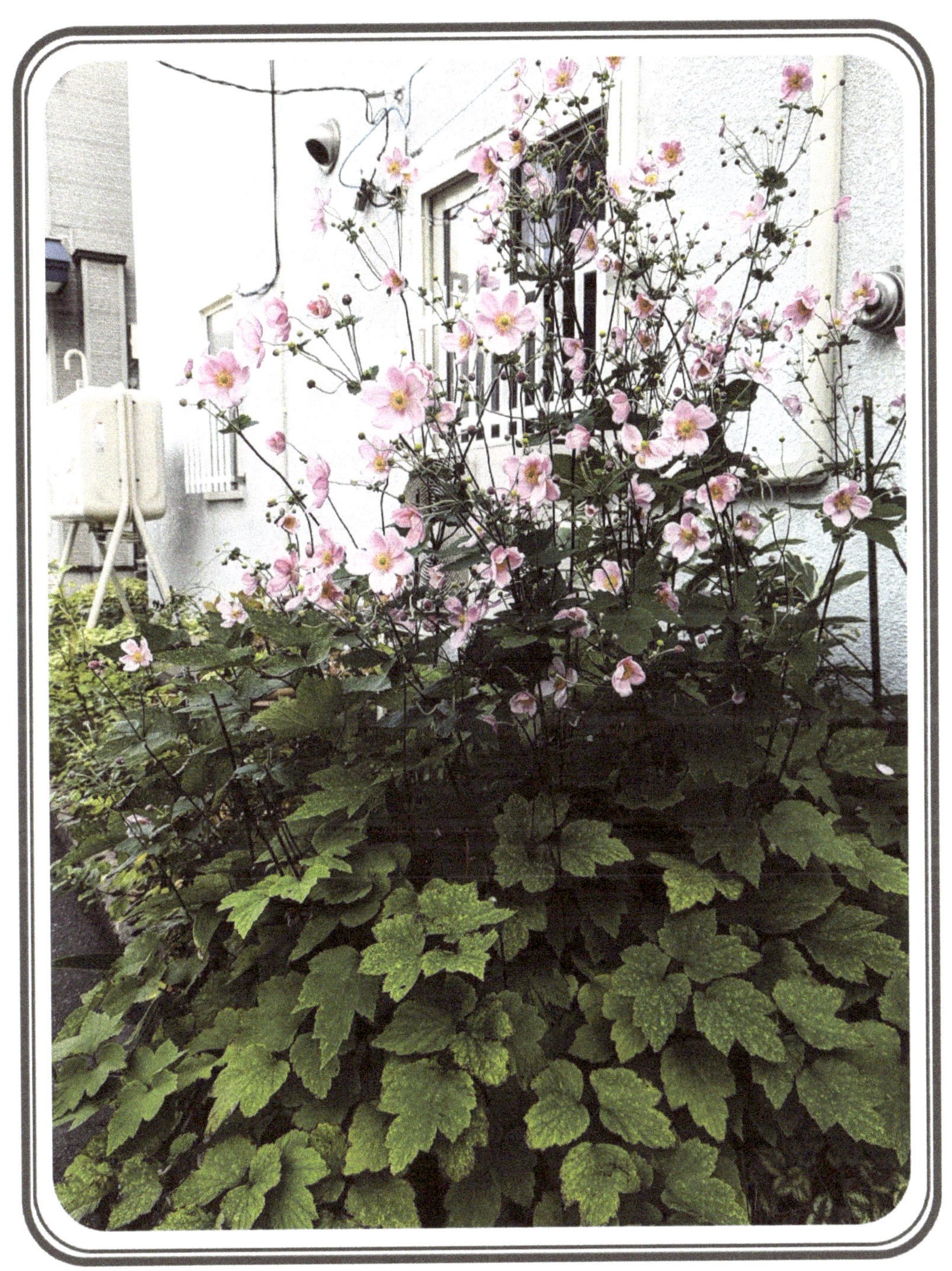

MYSTERIOUS

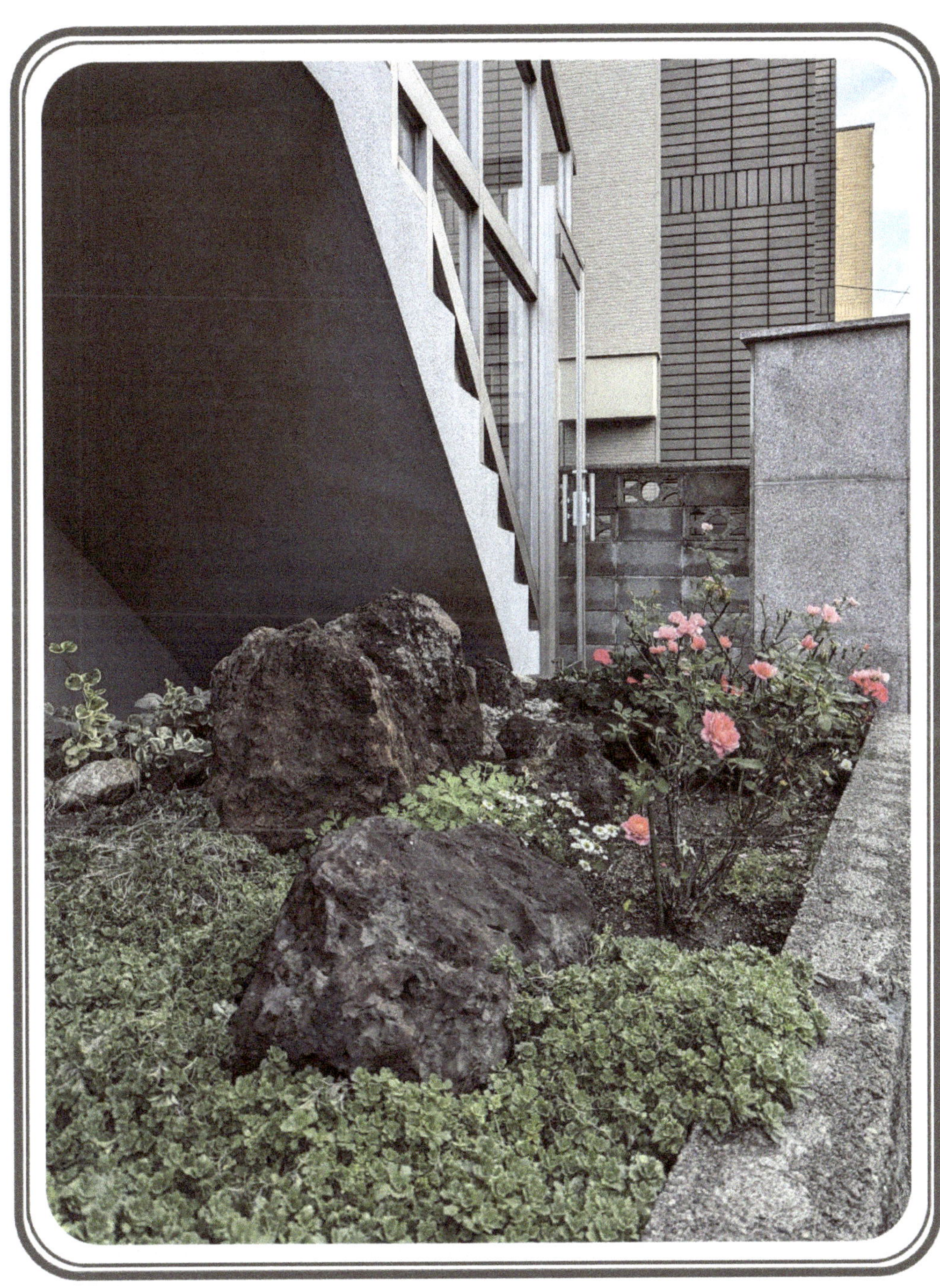

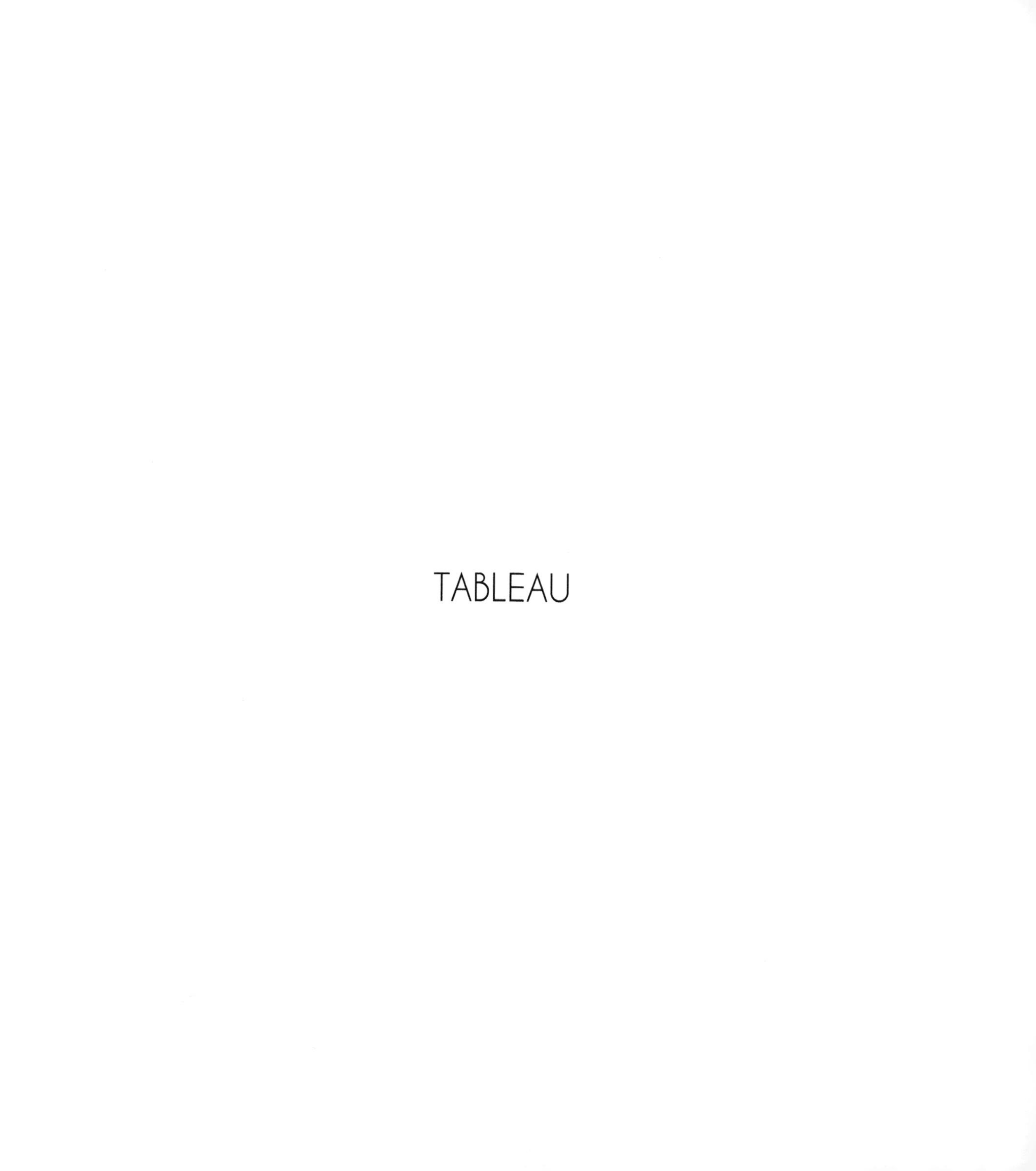
TABLEAU

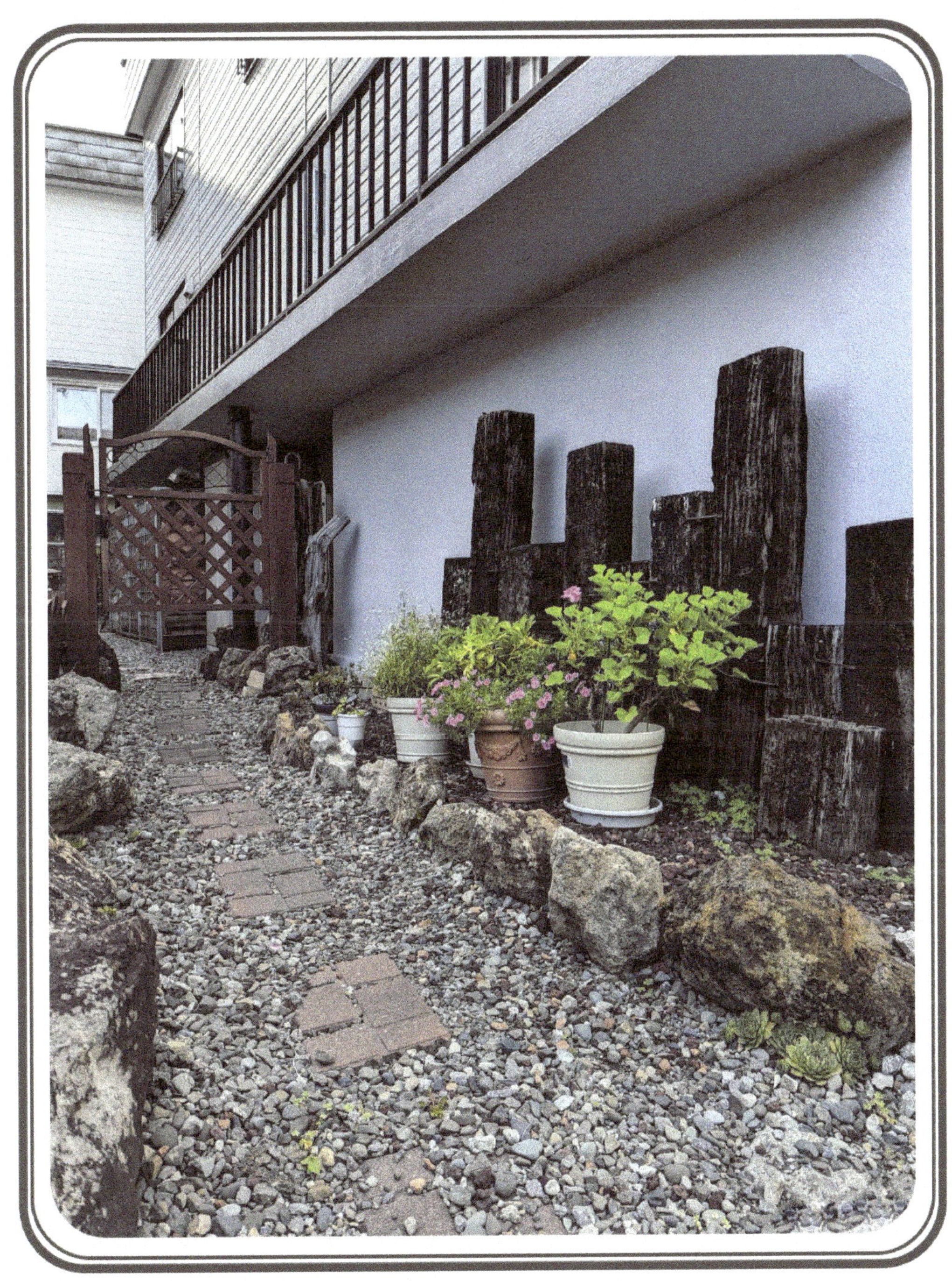

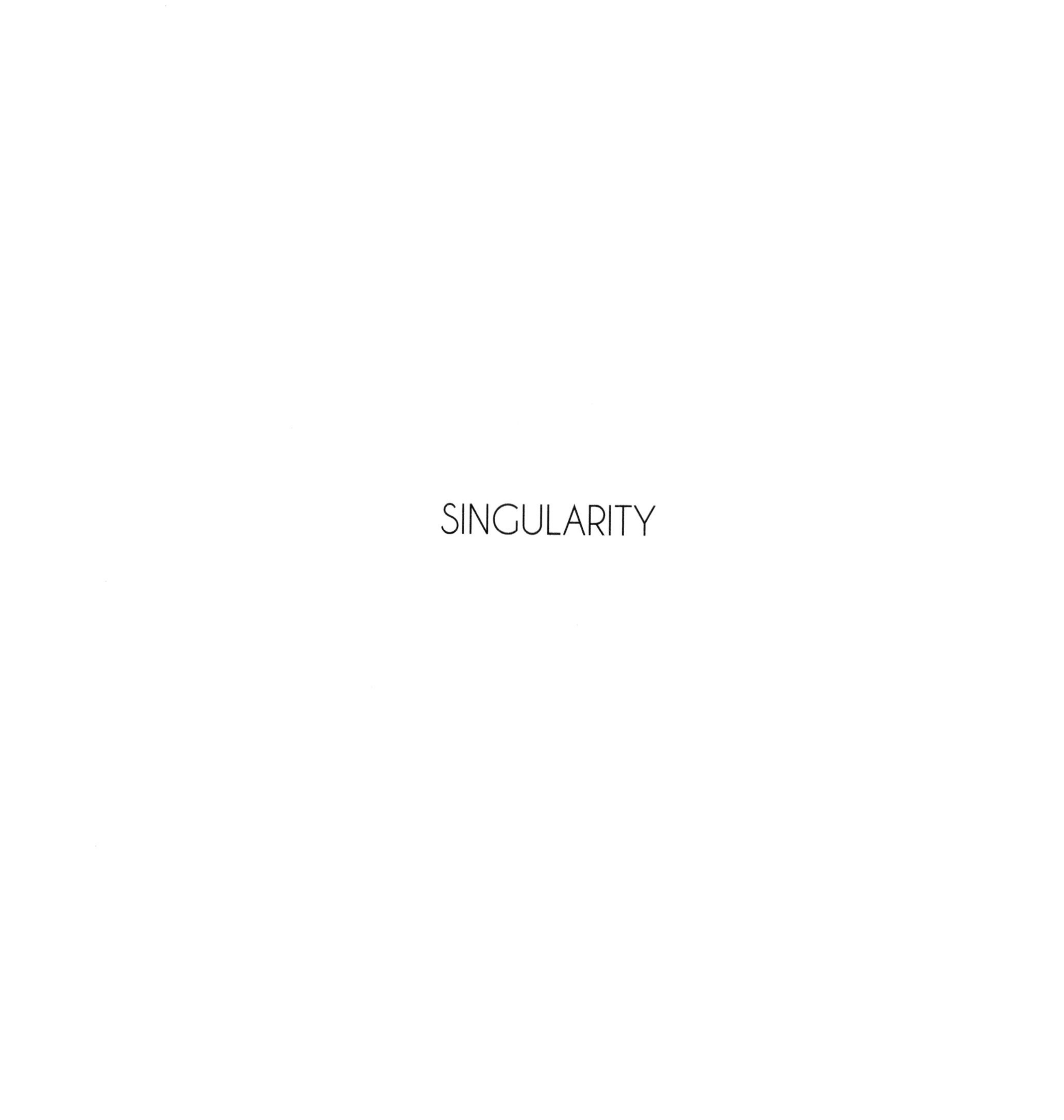

SINGULARITY

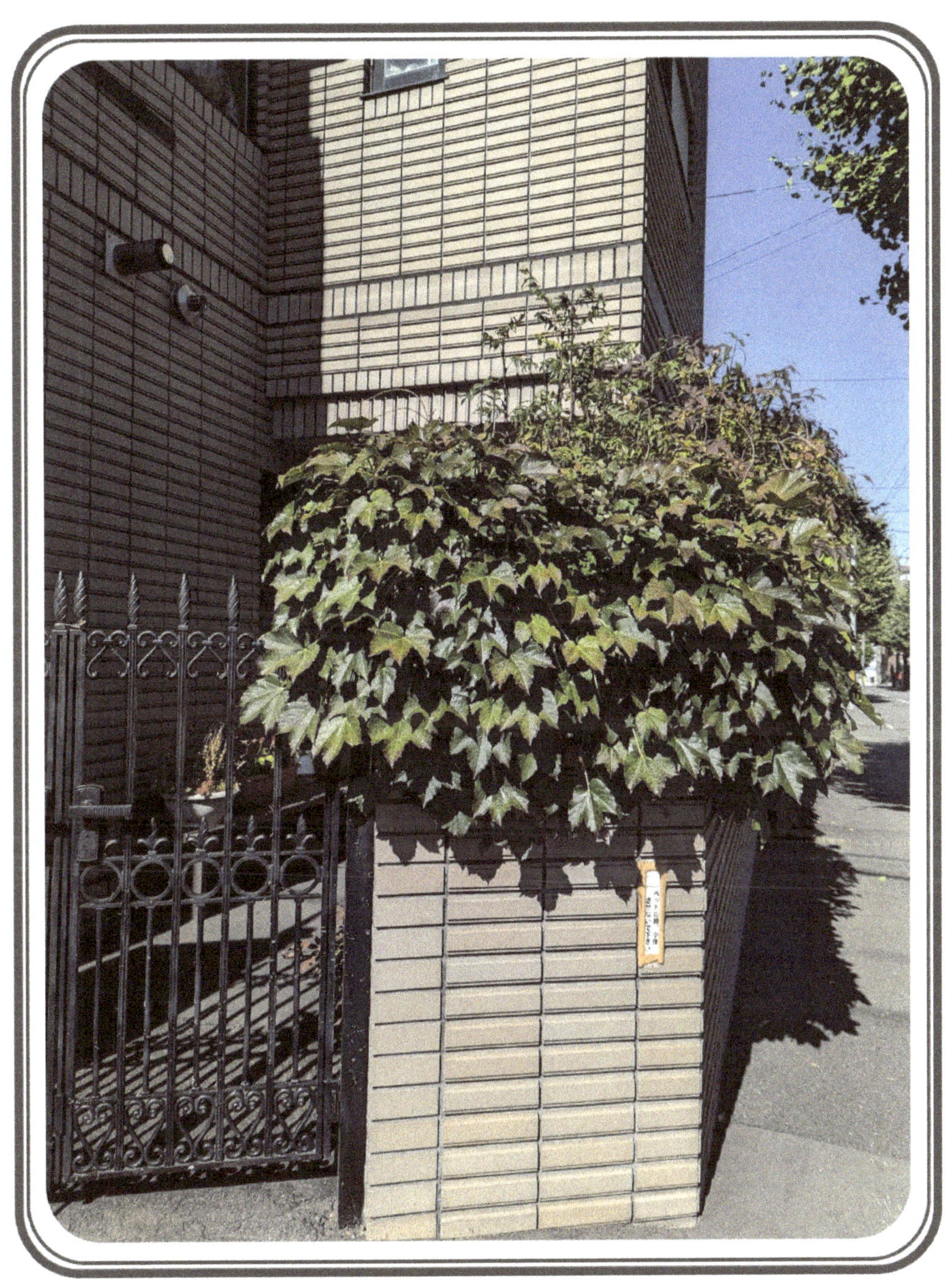

RUNAWAY

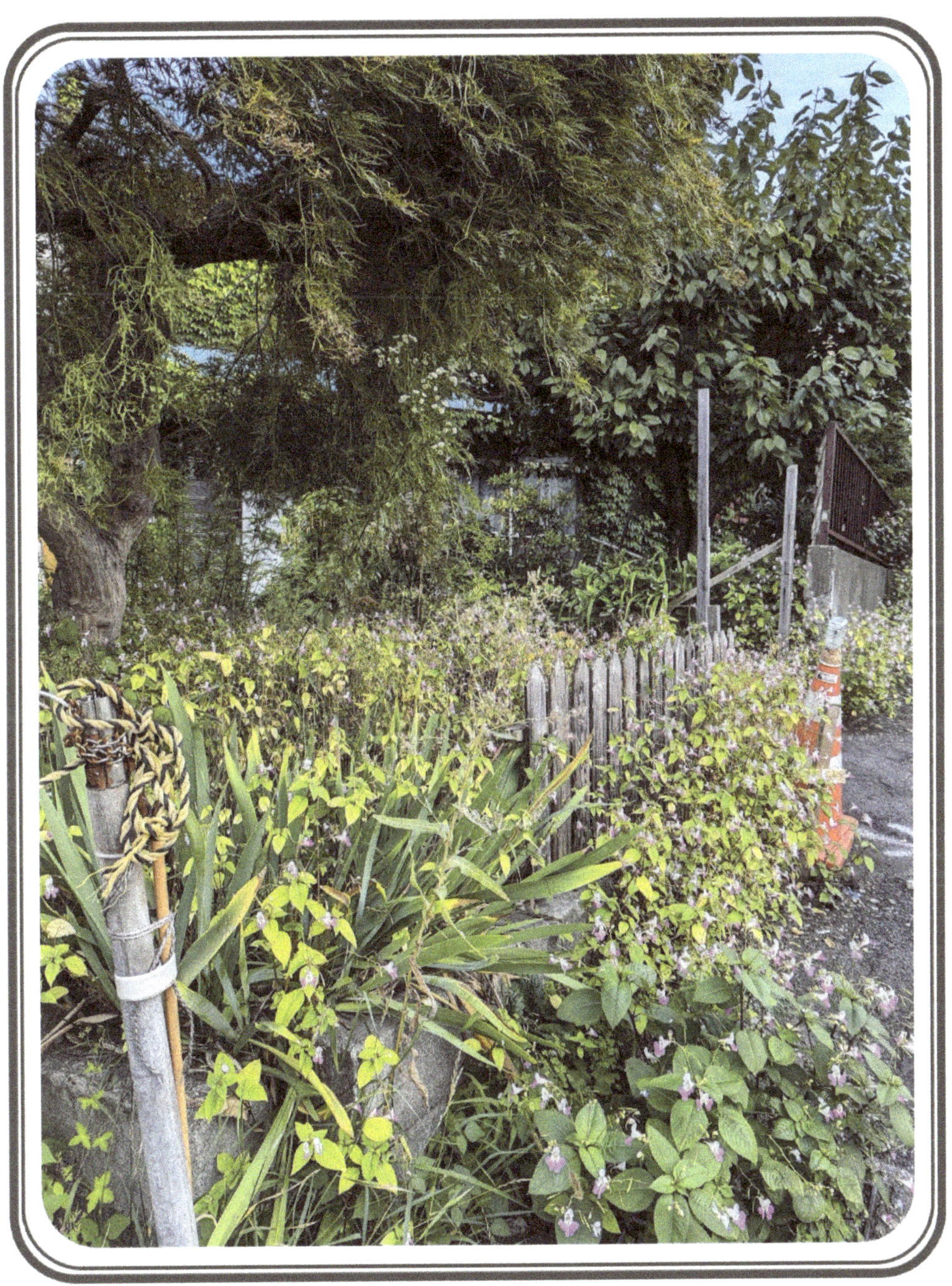

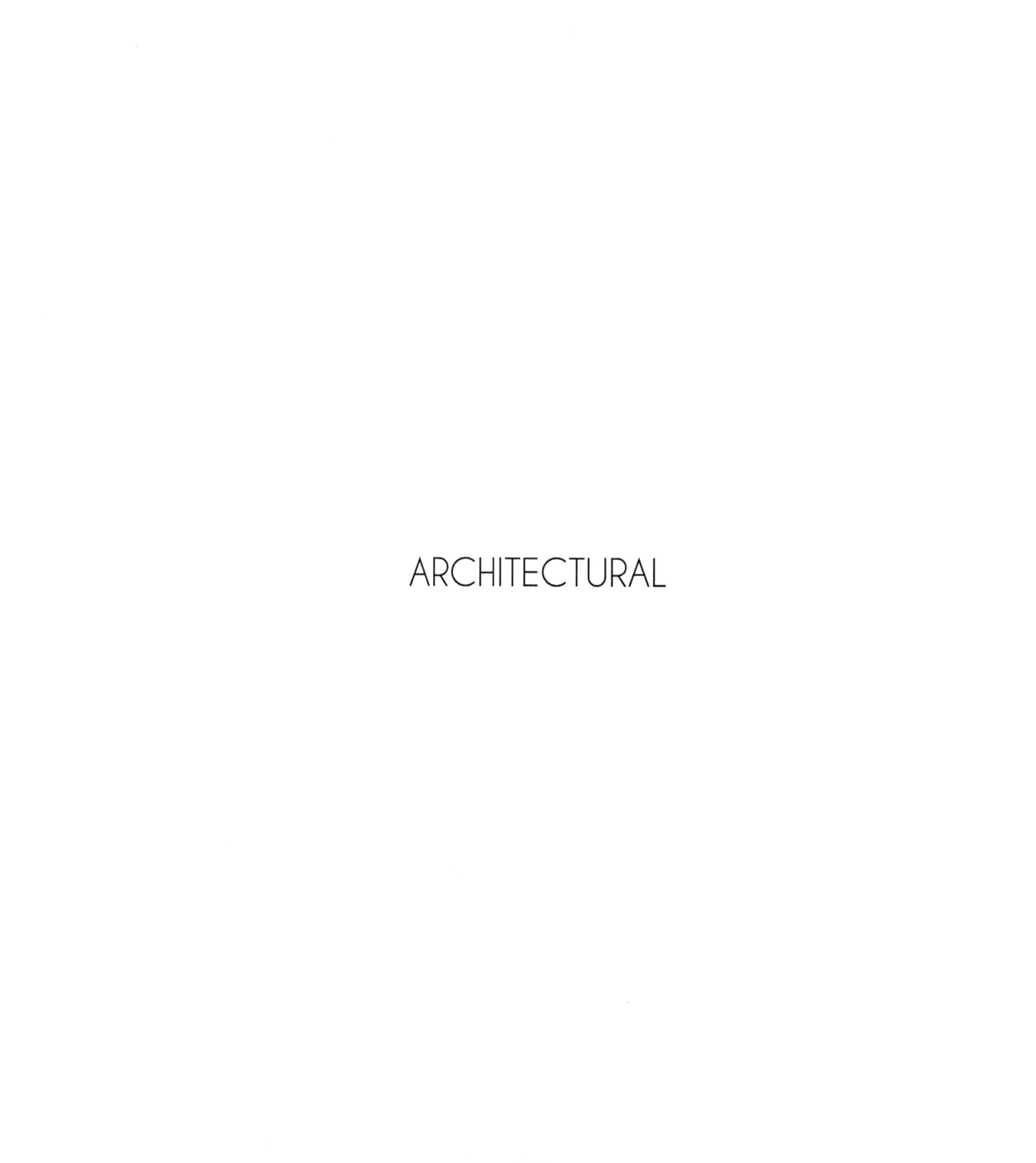

ARCHITECTURAL

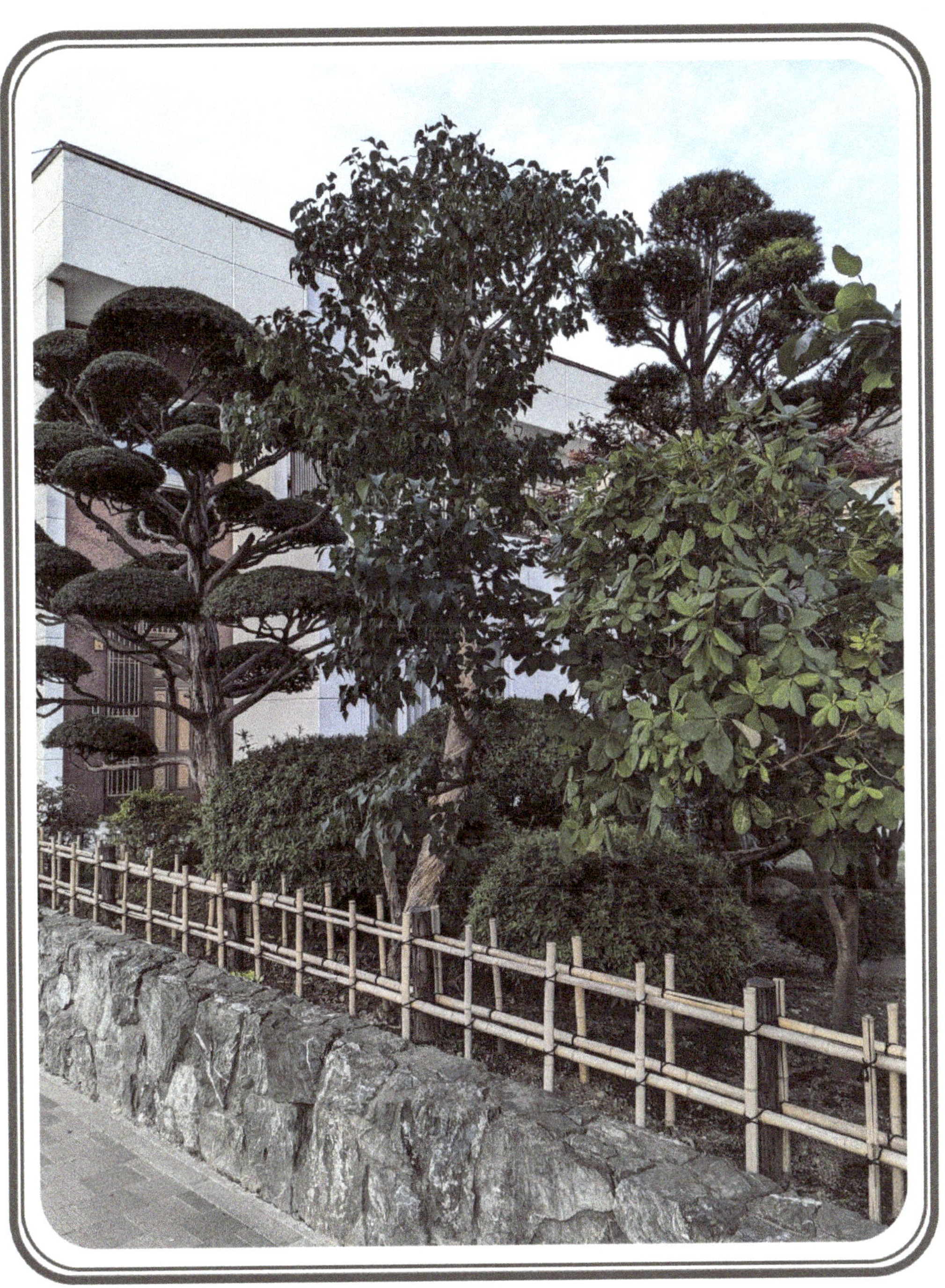

LAMINA

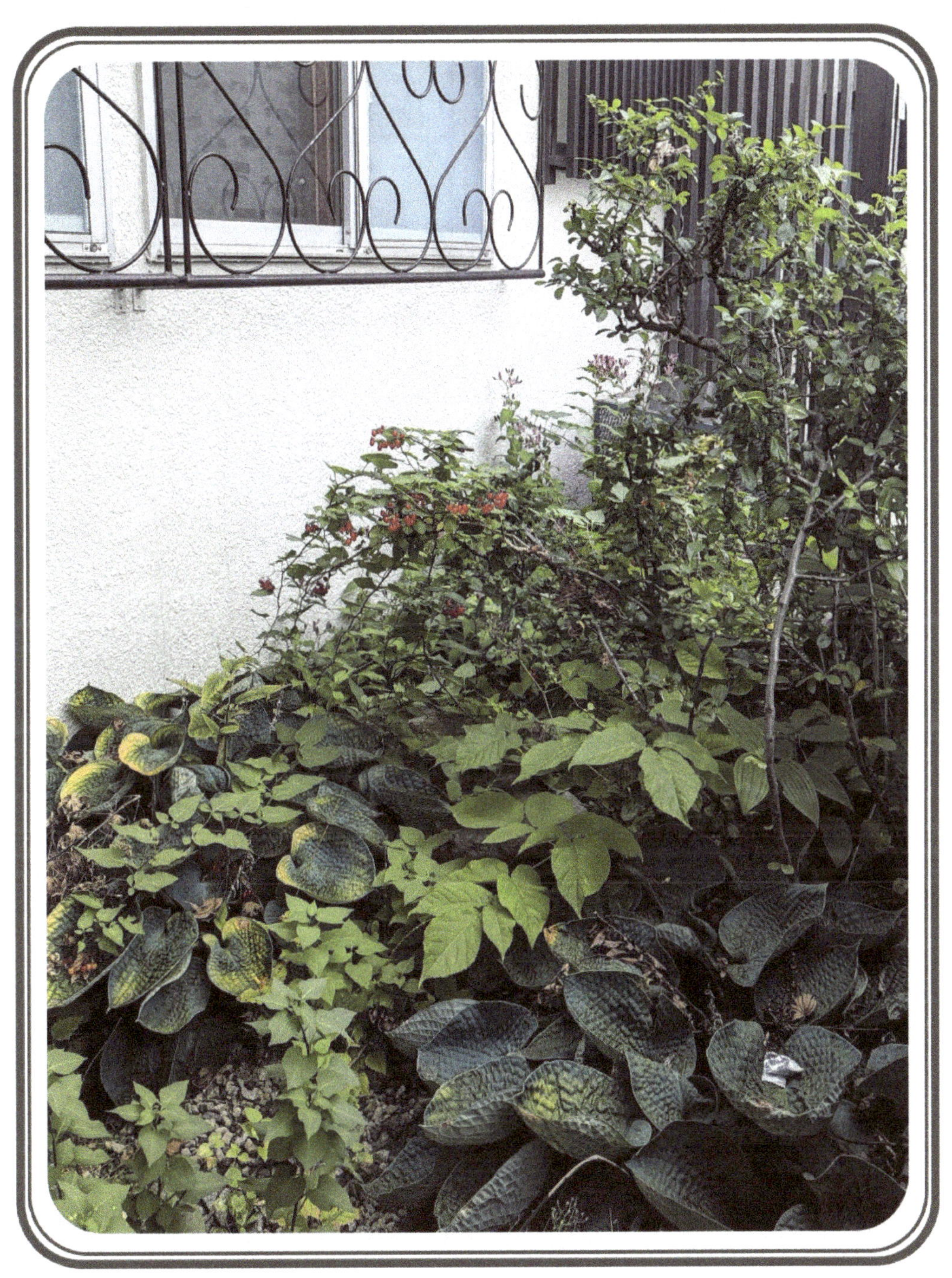

CLIFFSIDE

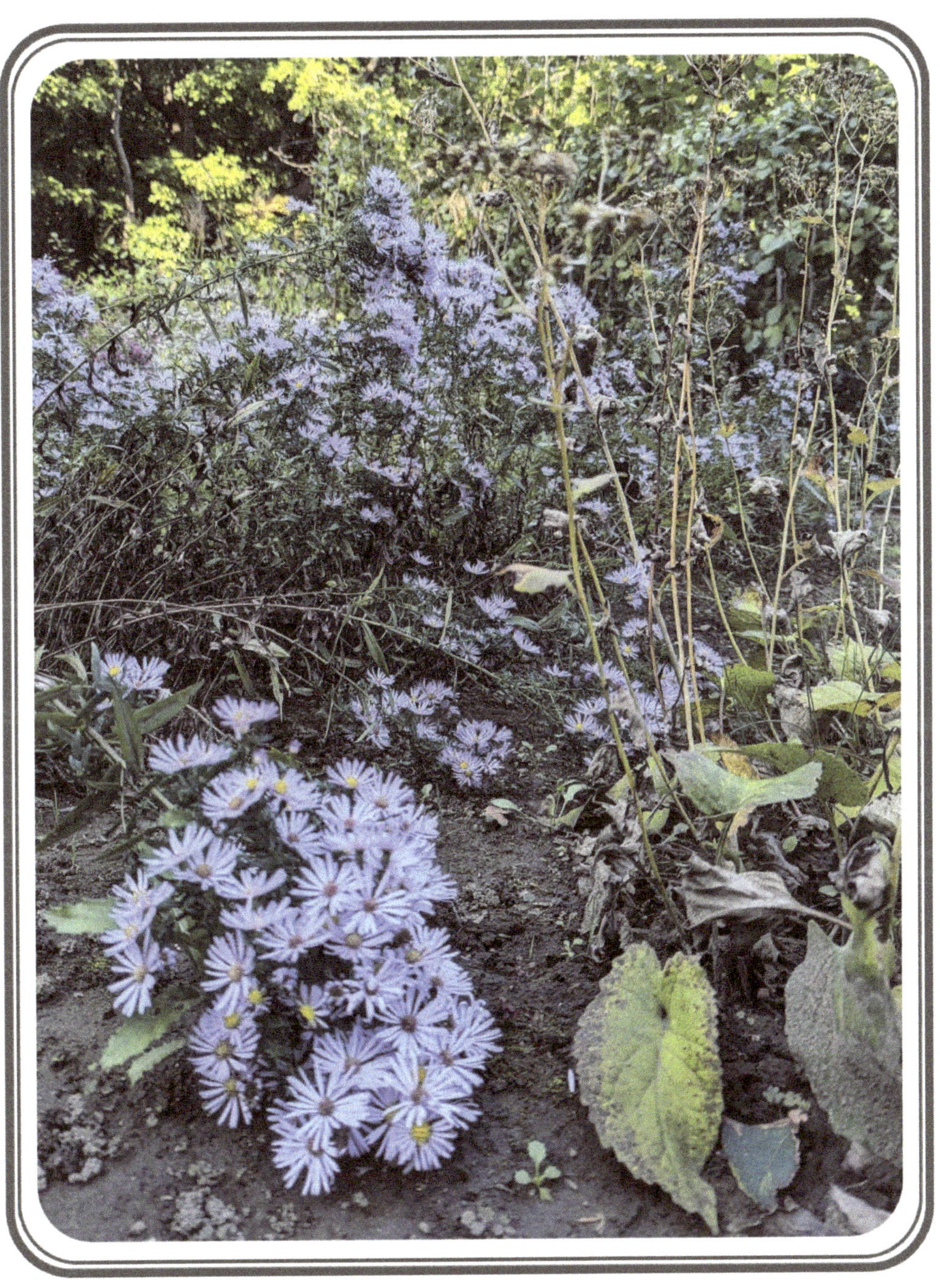

IGNITION

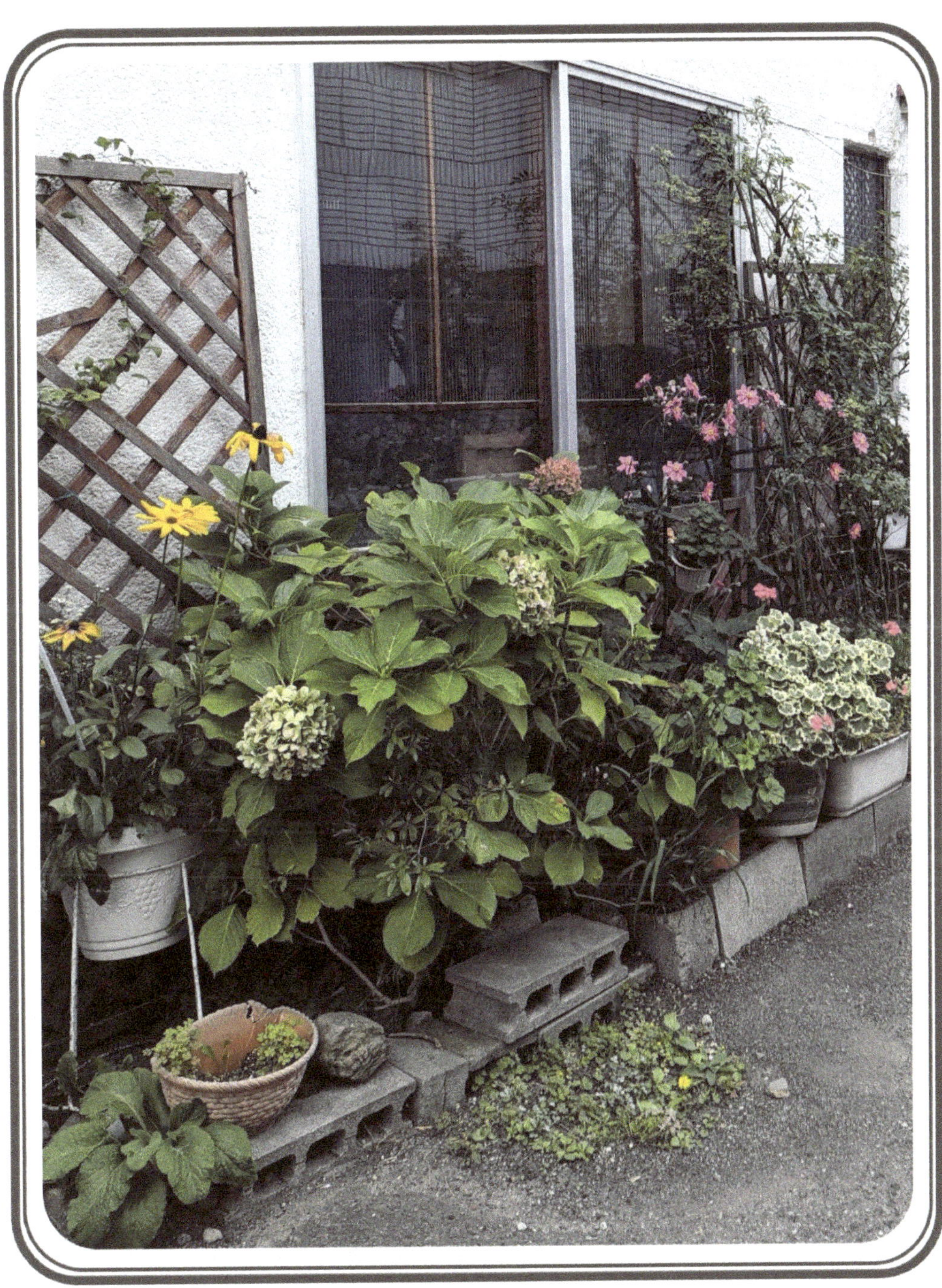

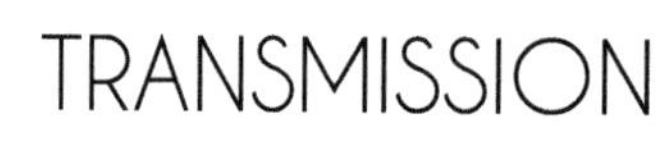
TRANSMISSION

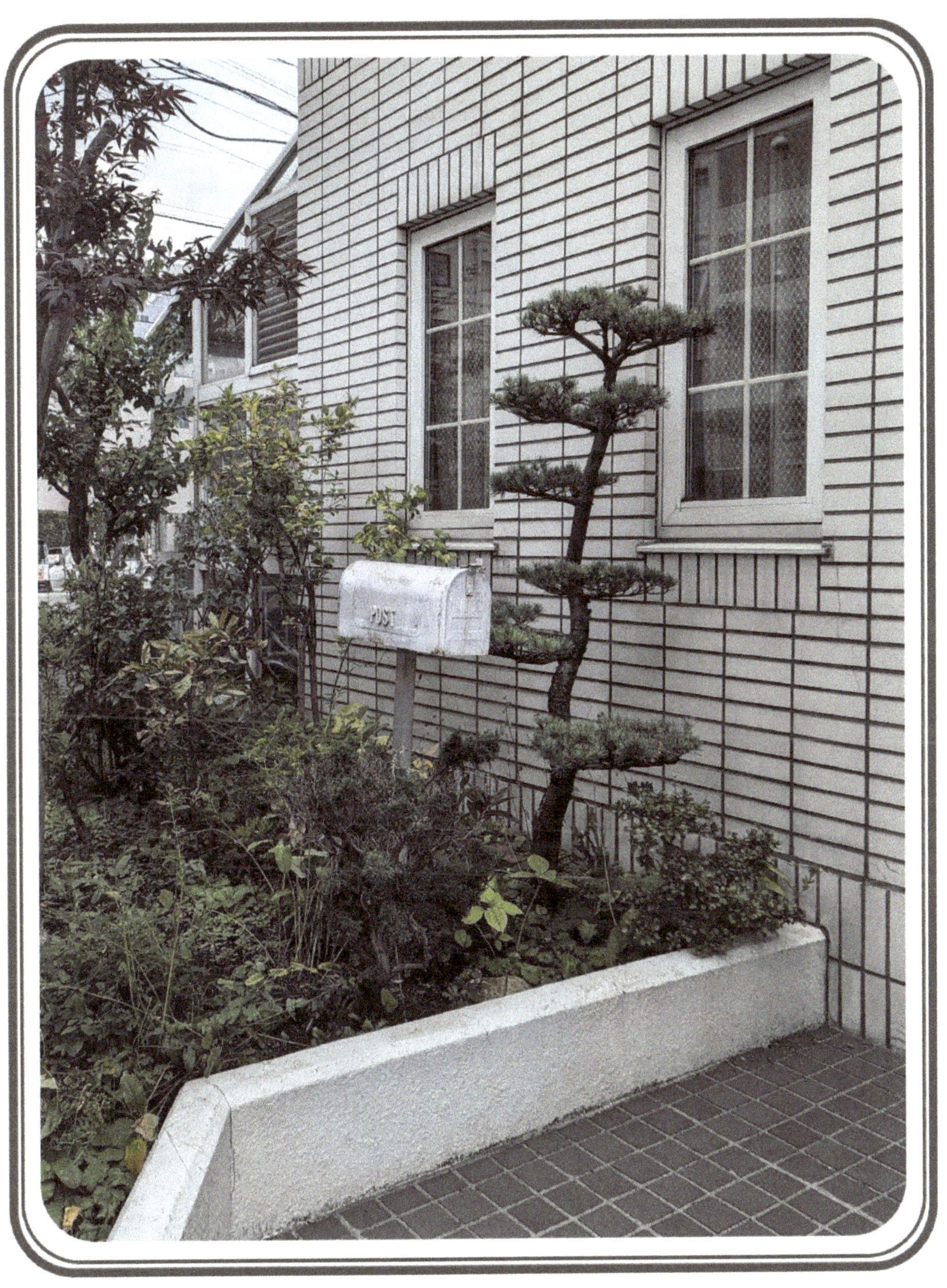
POST

THIMBLE

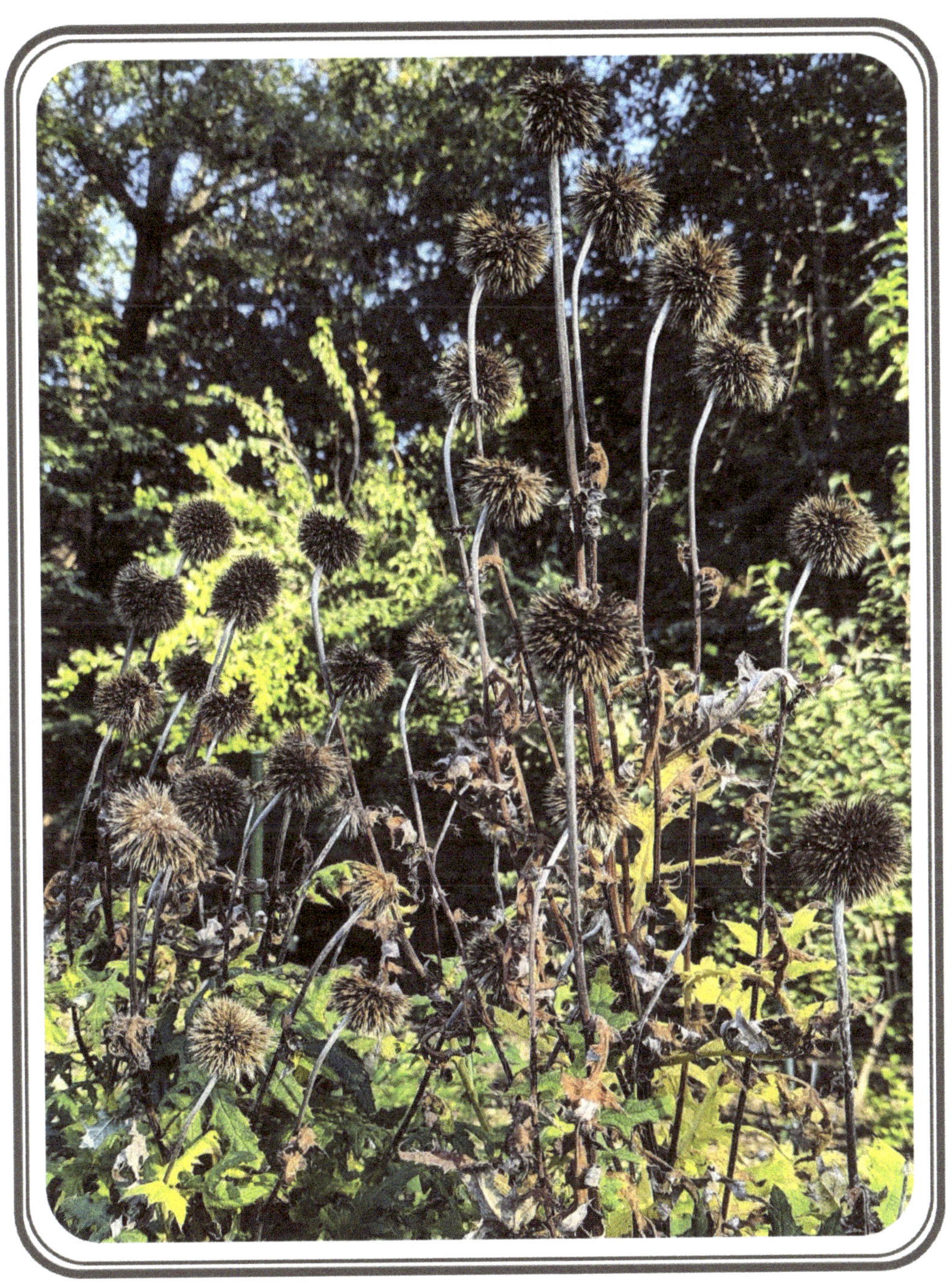

YAWP

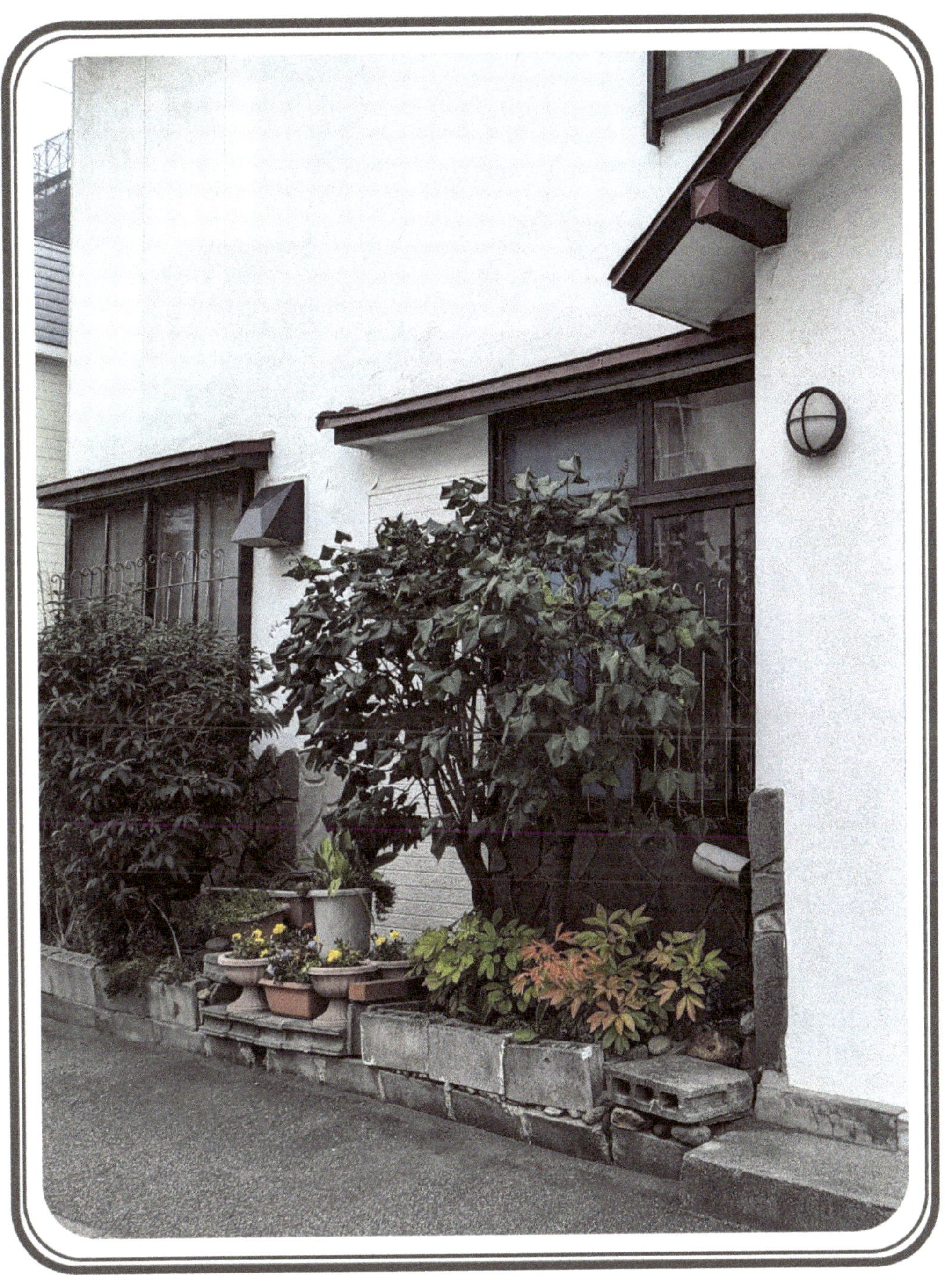

GRUMBLE

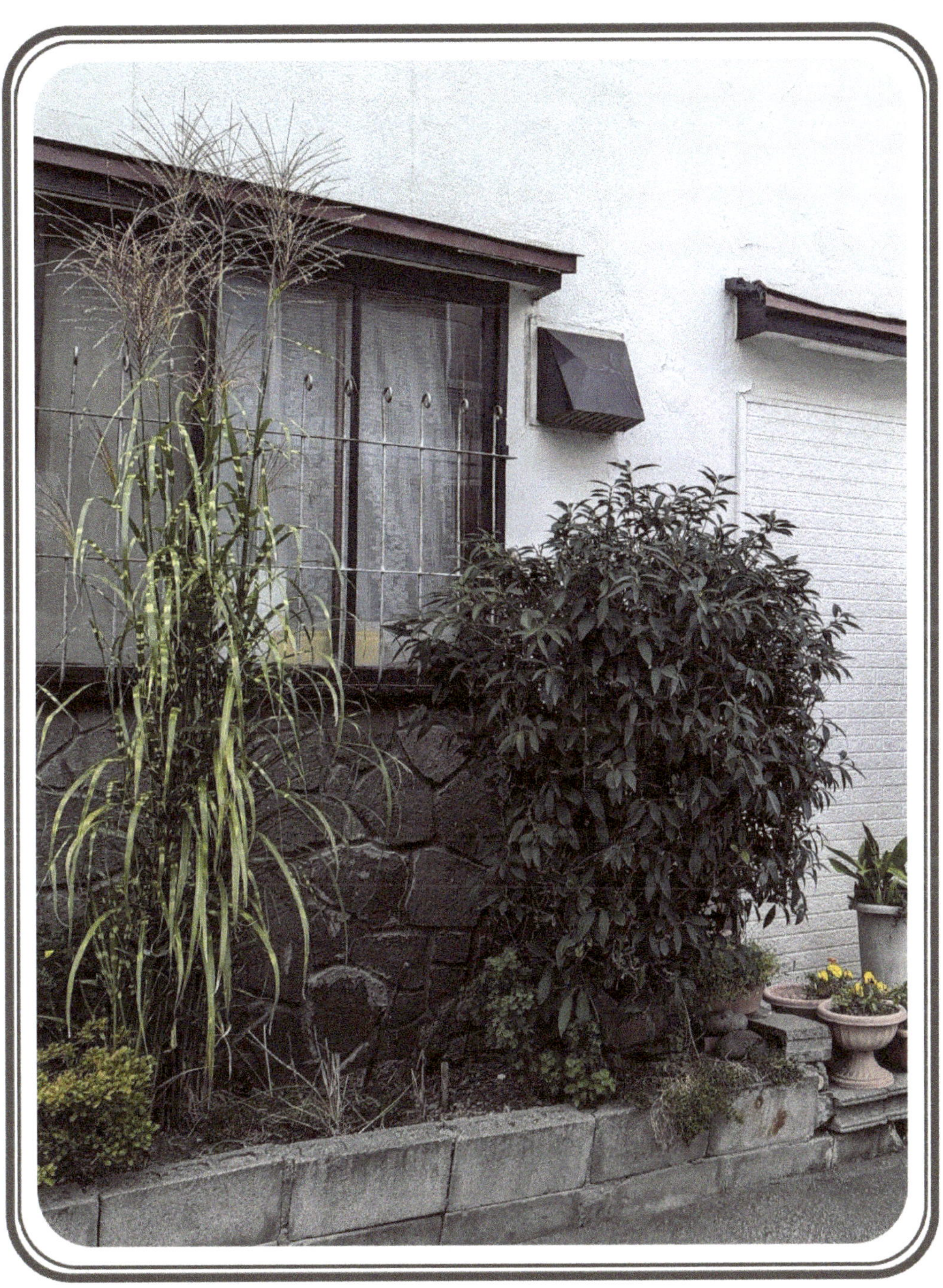

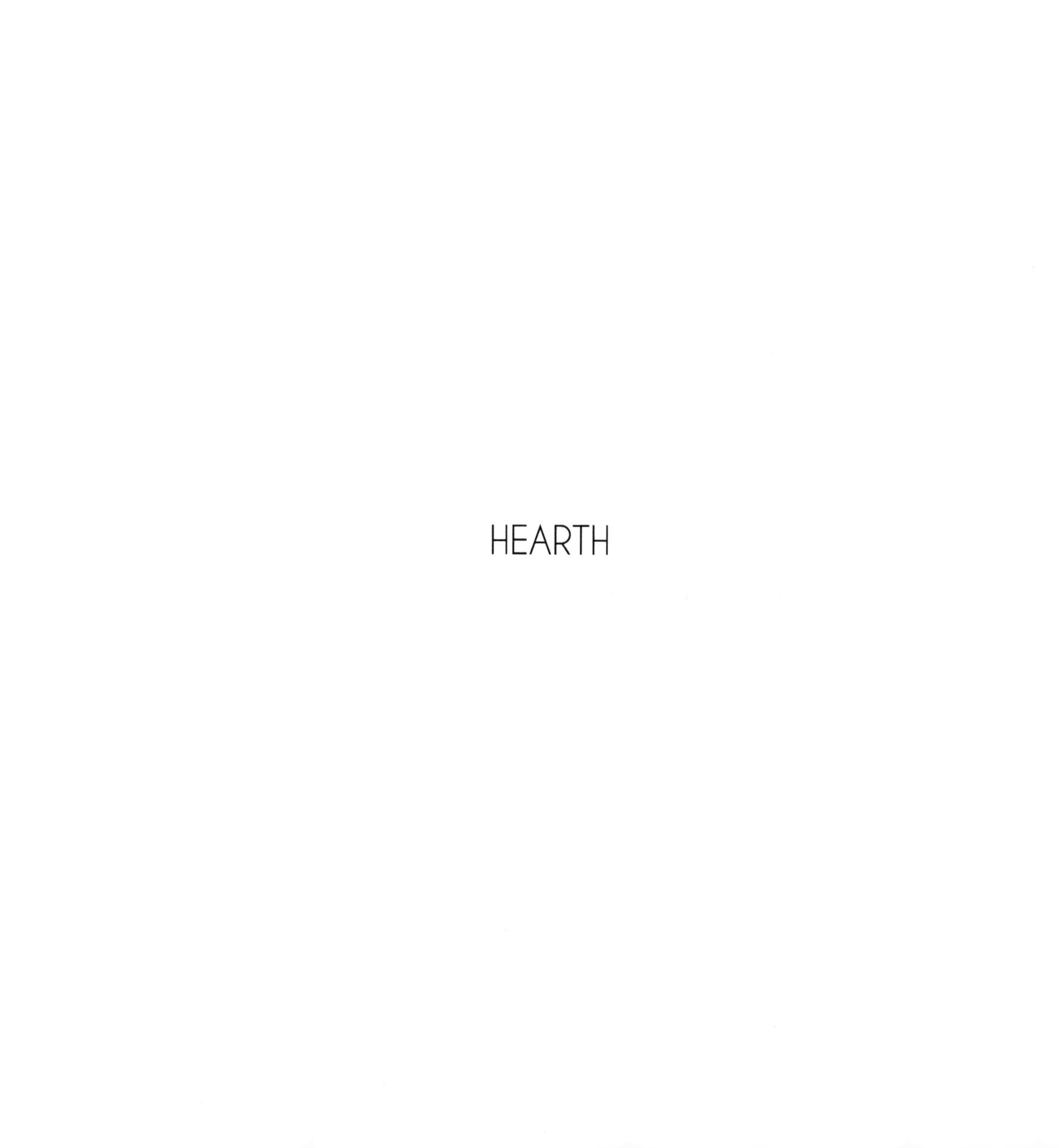

HEARTH

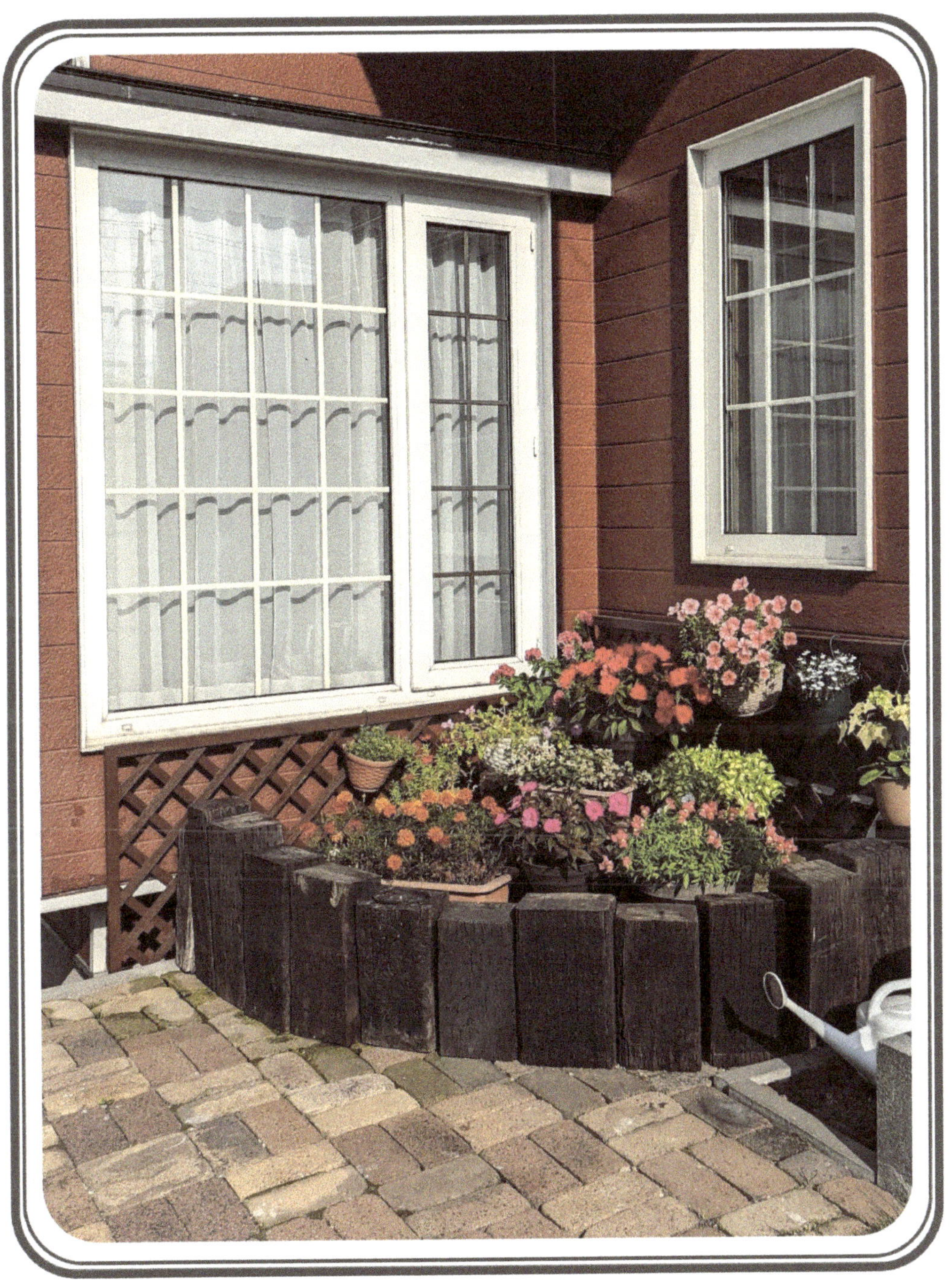

GNOME

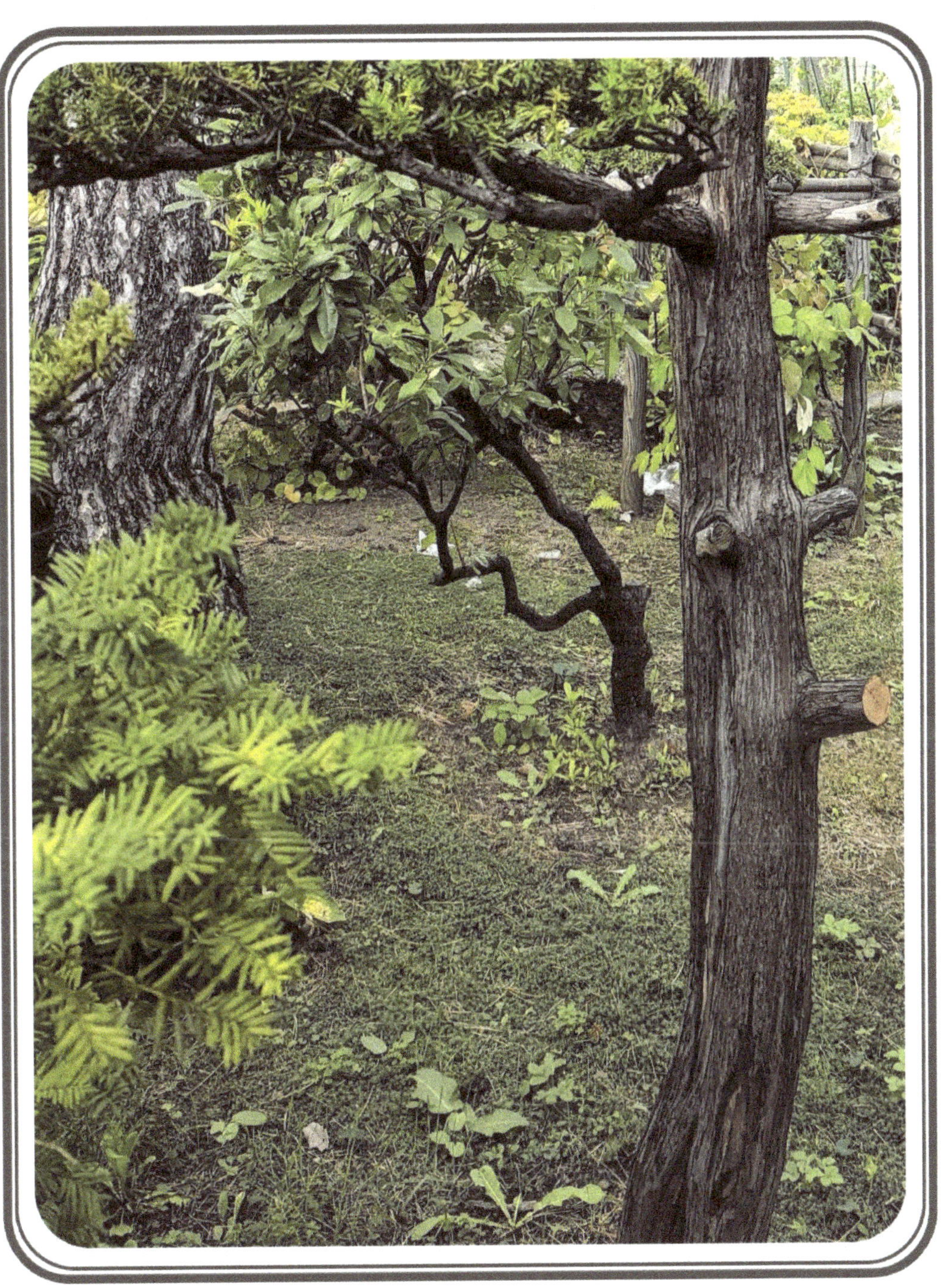

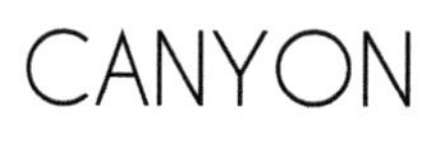
CANYON

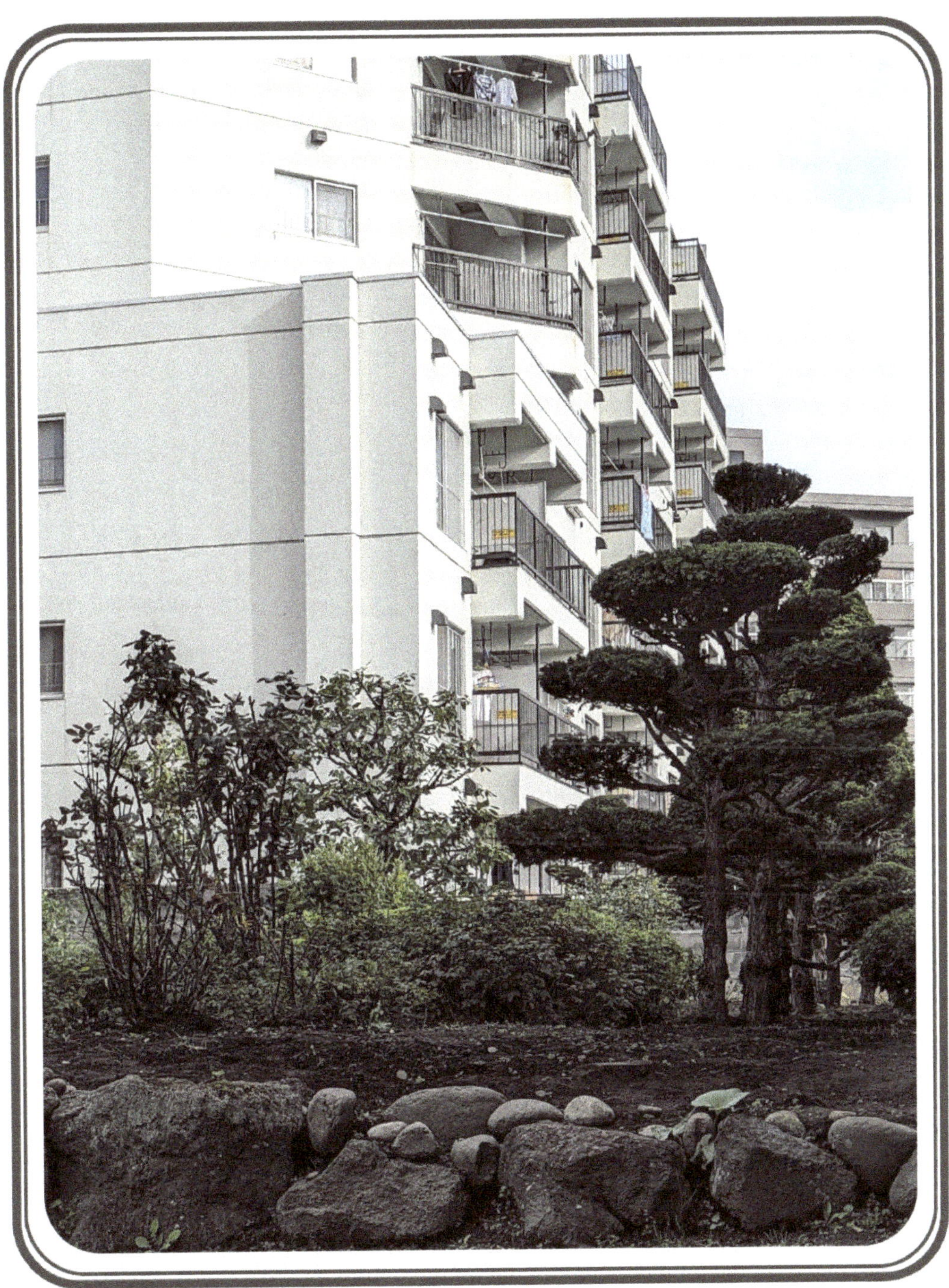

WAVER

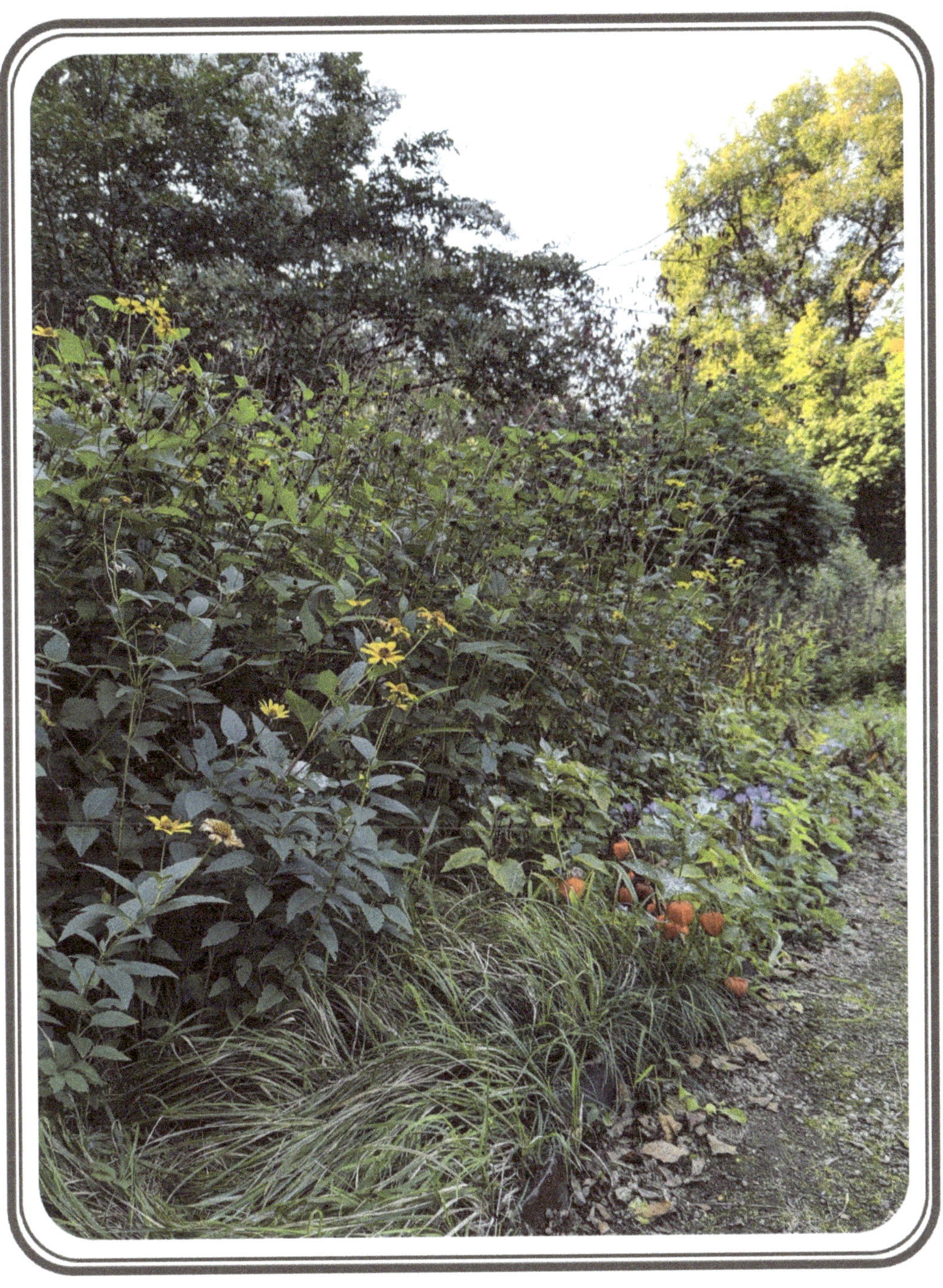

SPRINKLE

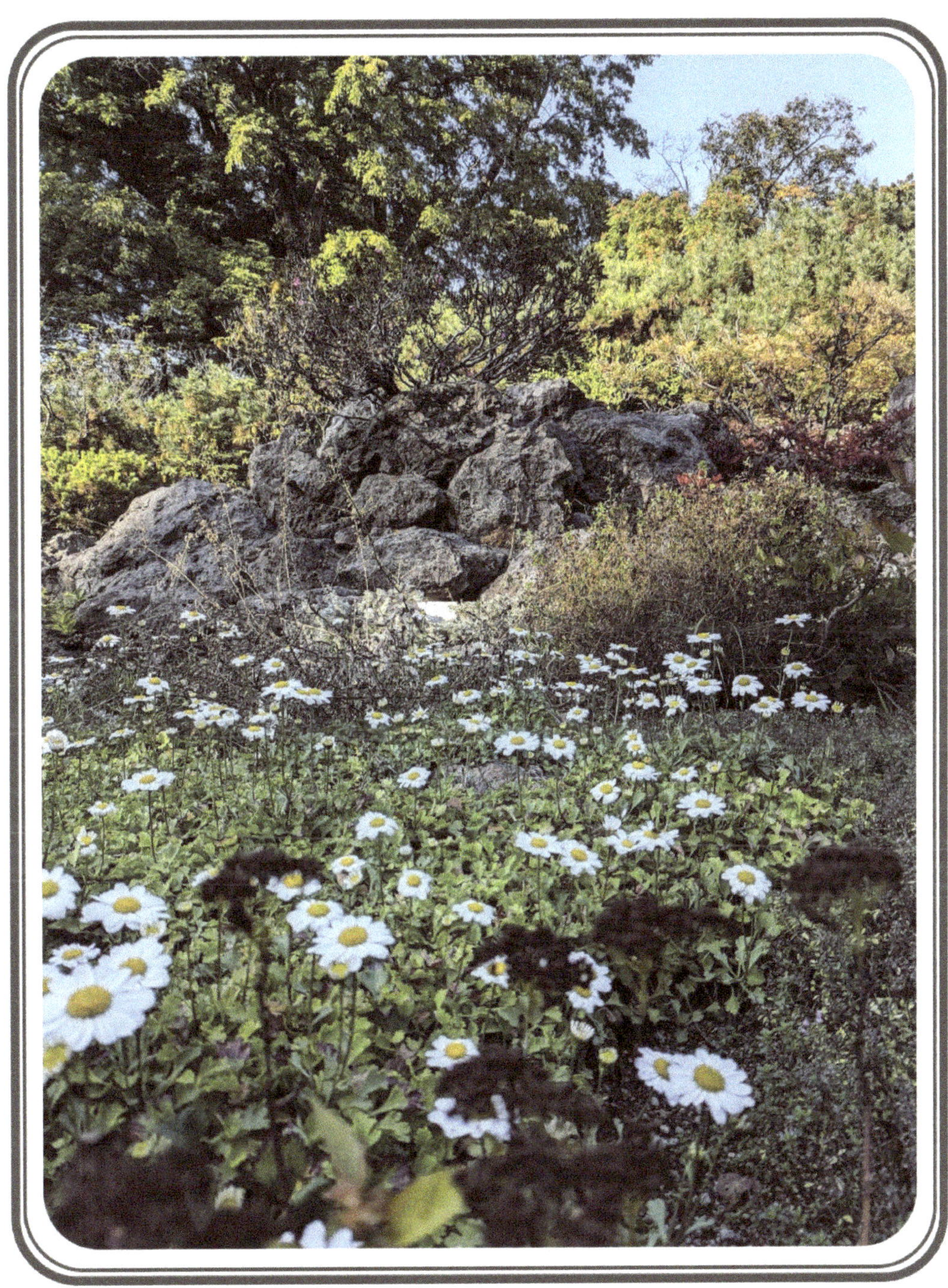

GIFT

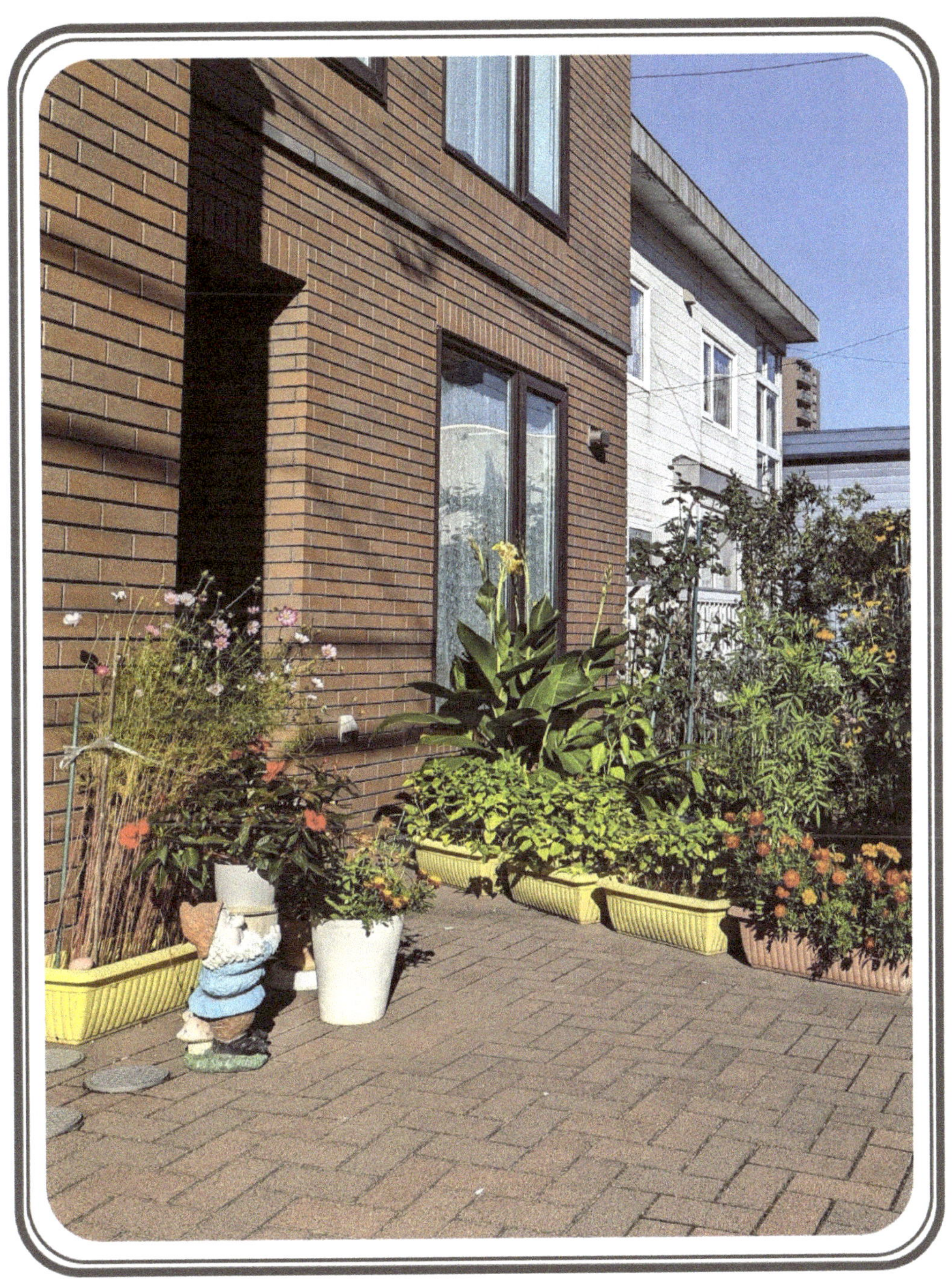

GRIFFIN

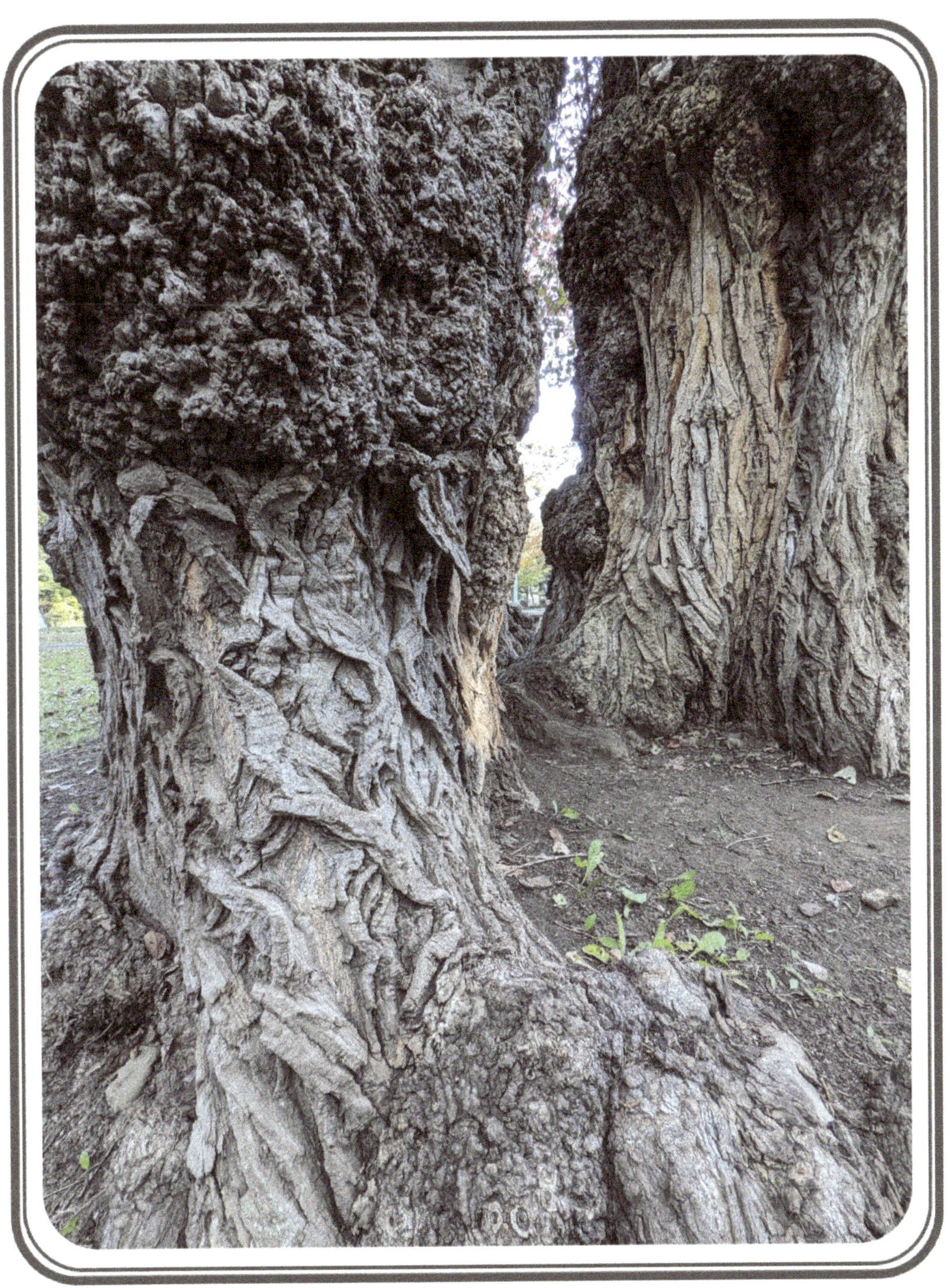

FLAGSTAFF

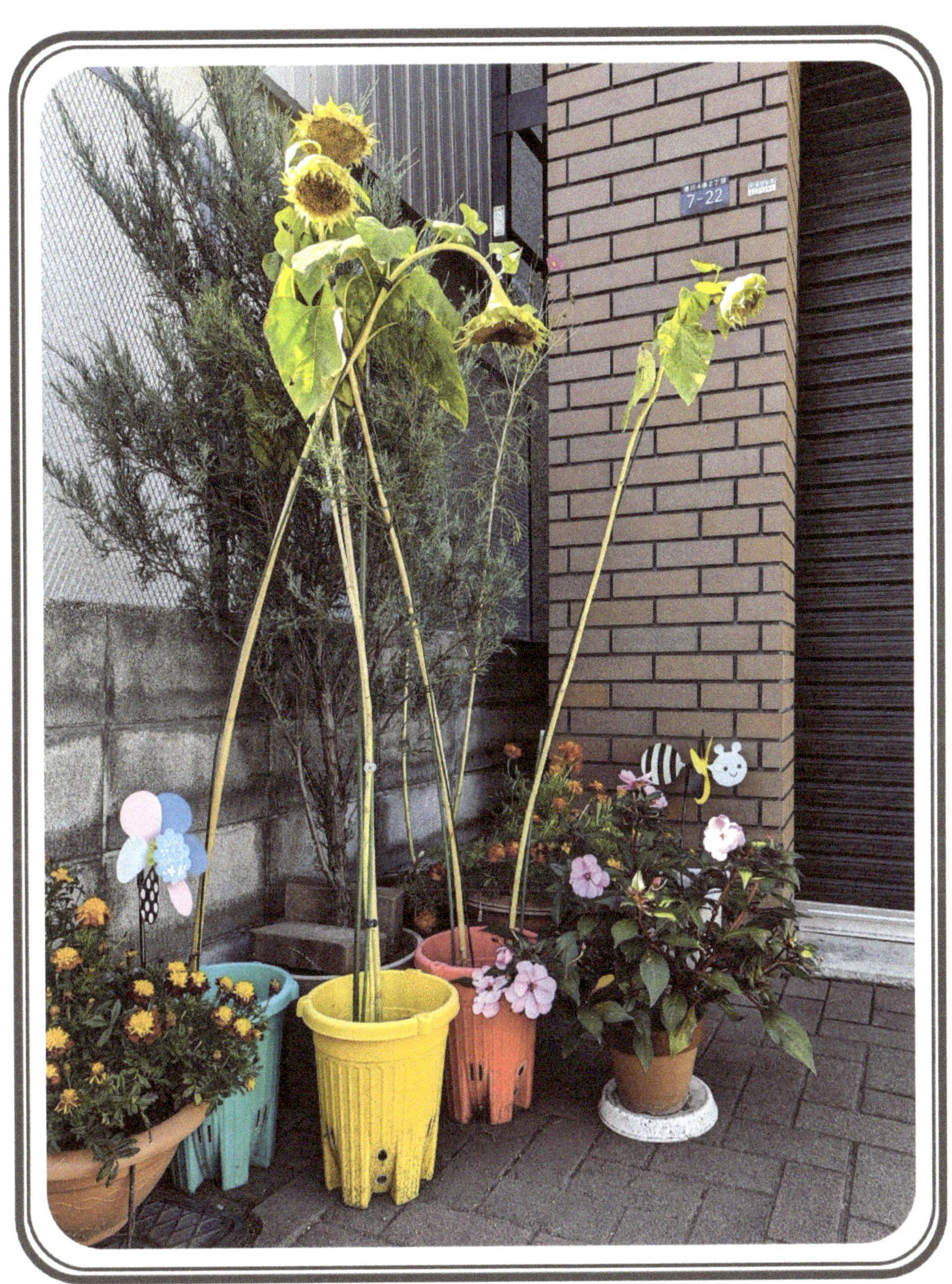
7-22

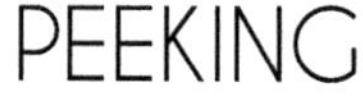
PEEKING

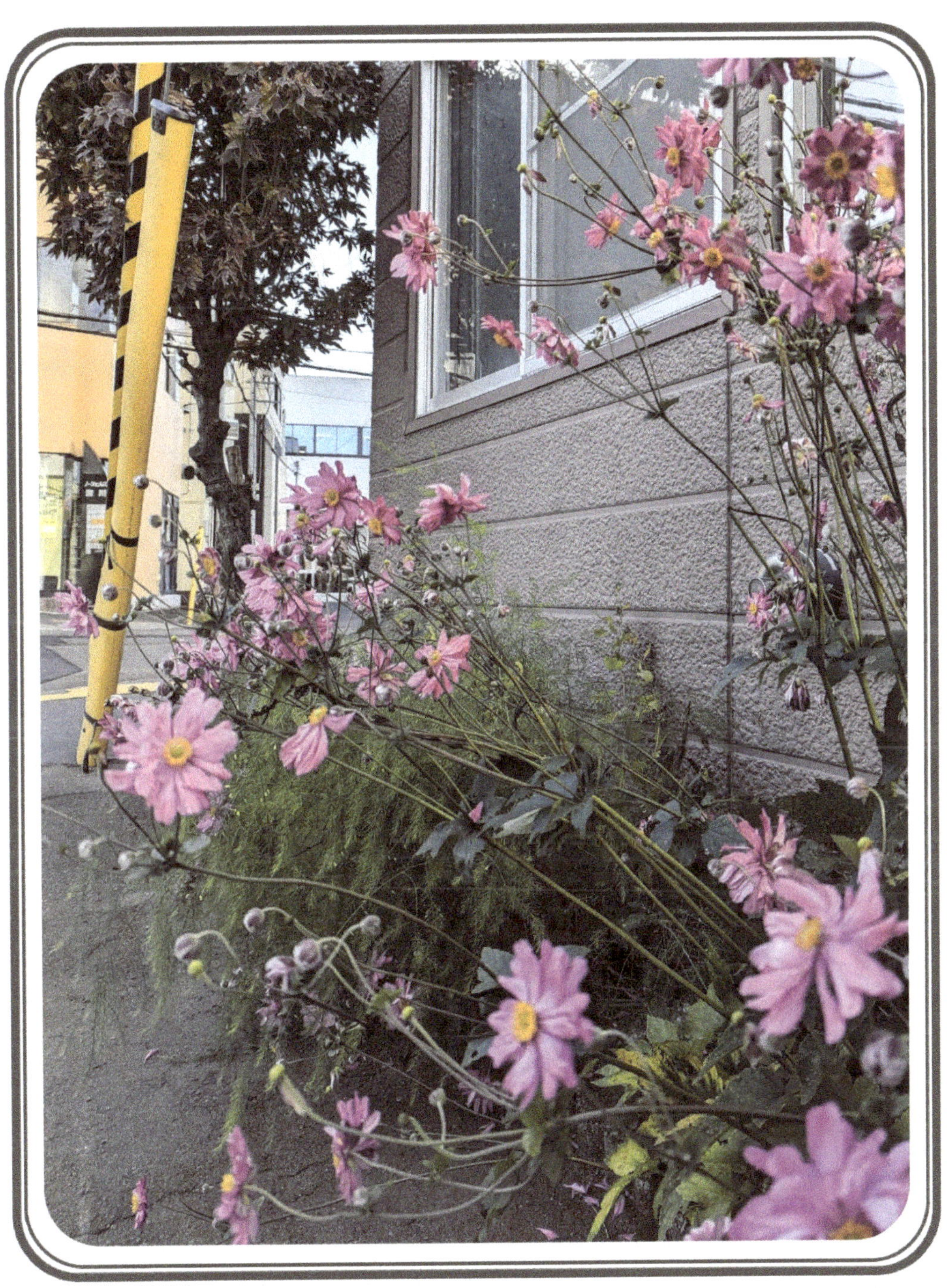

STOCK

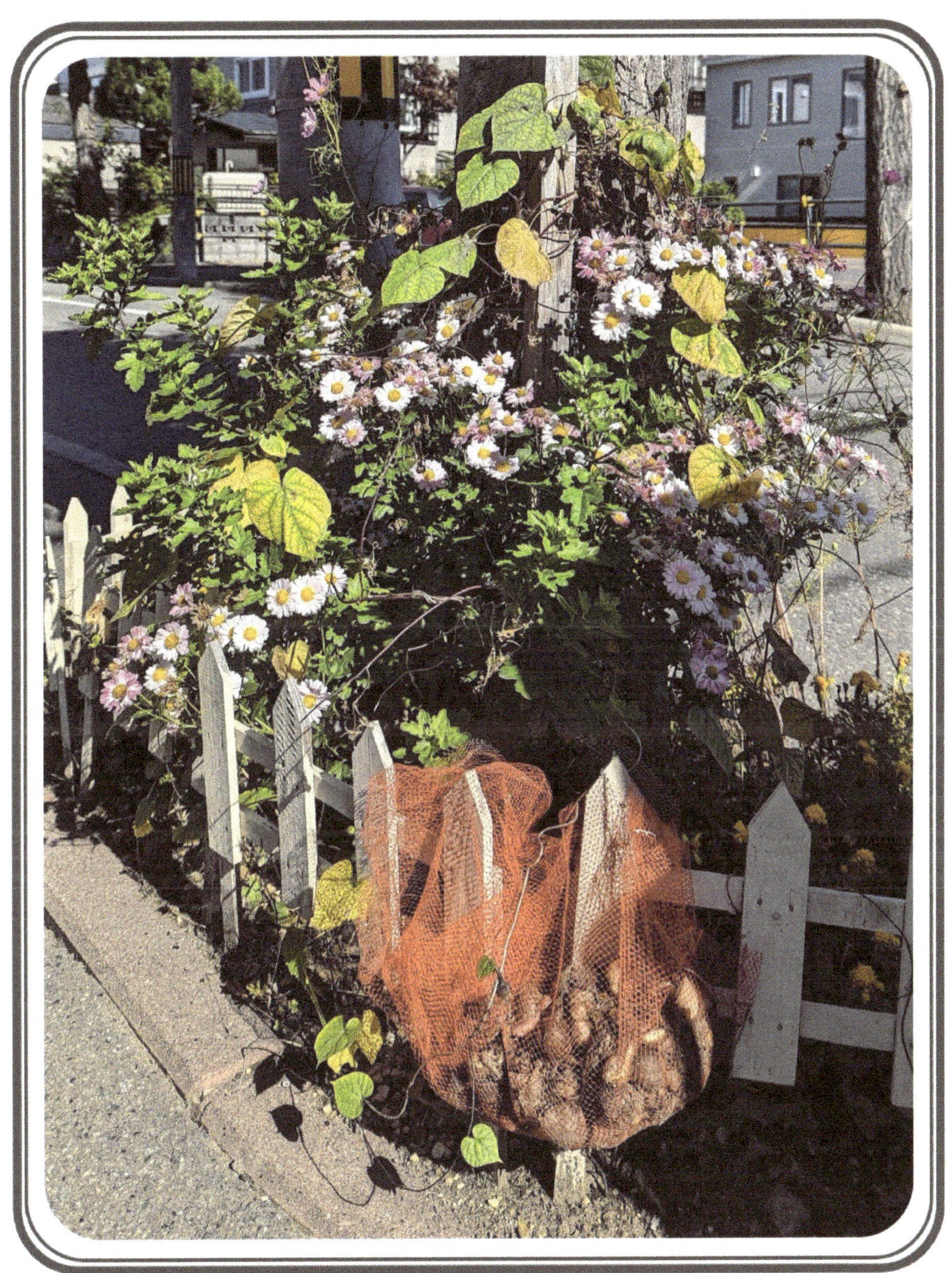

REEL

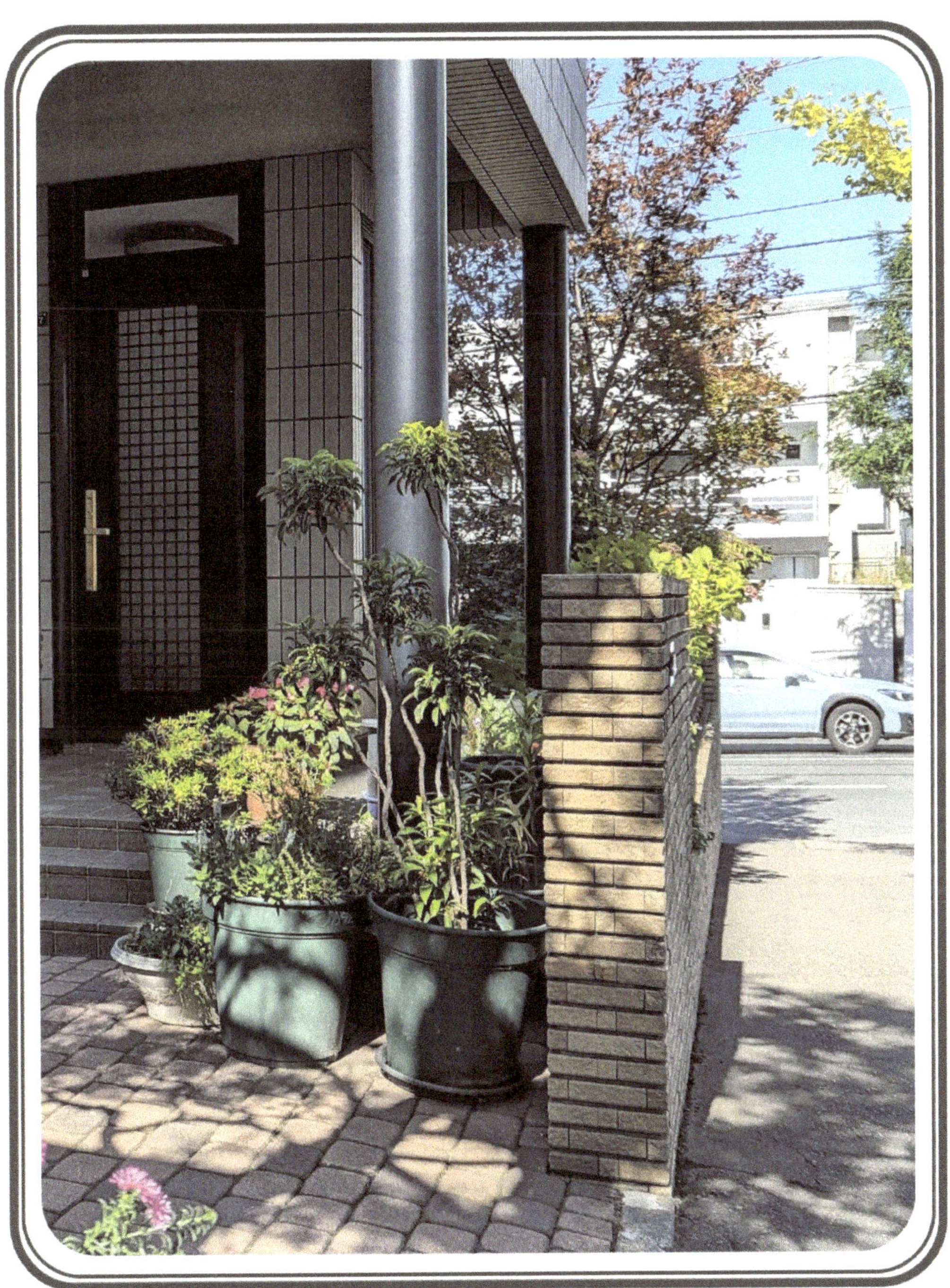

LAUNCH

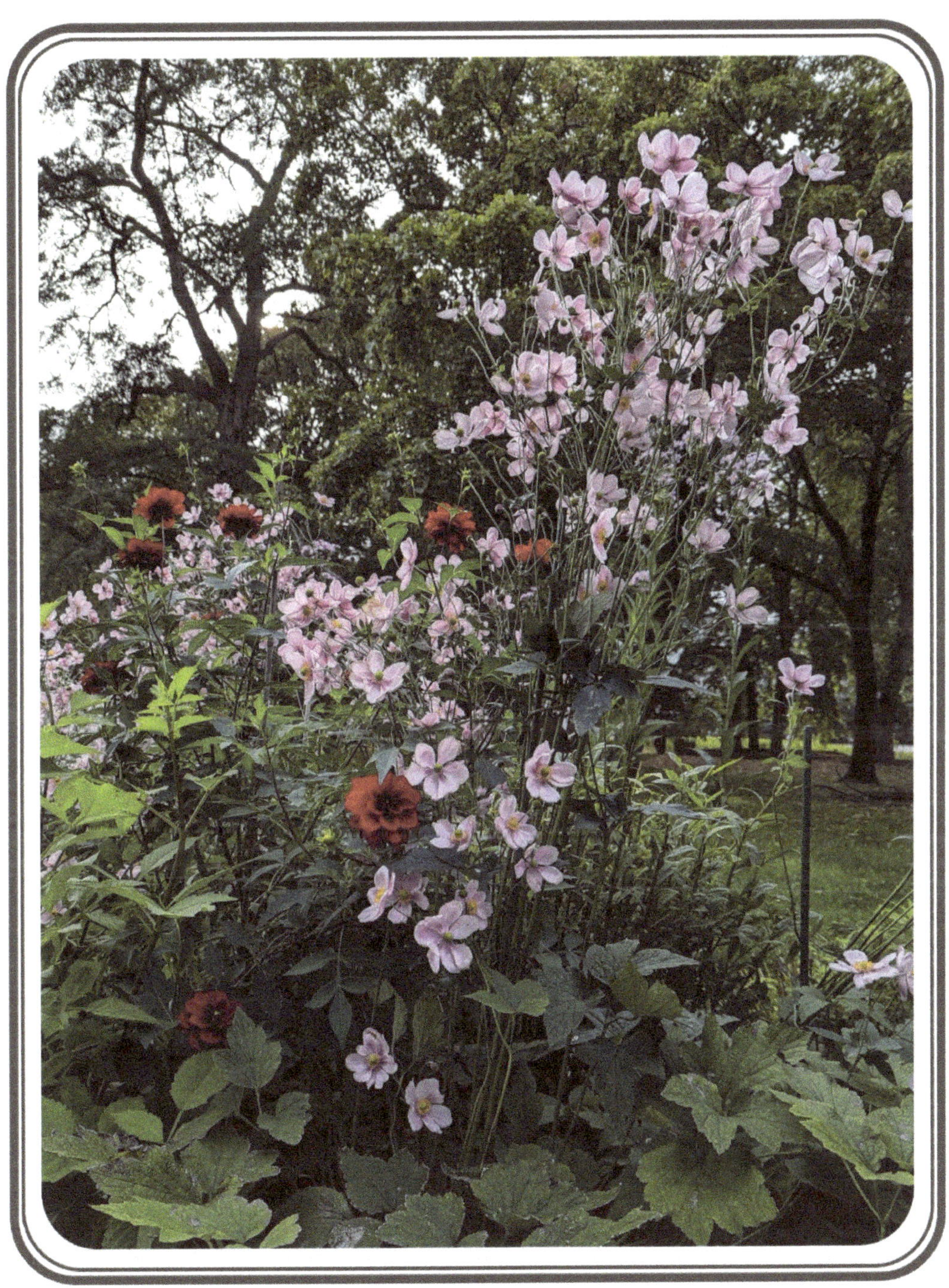

RETREAT

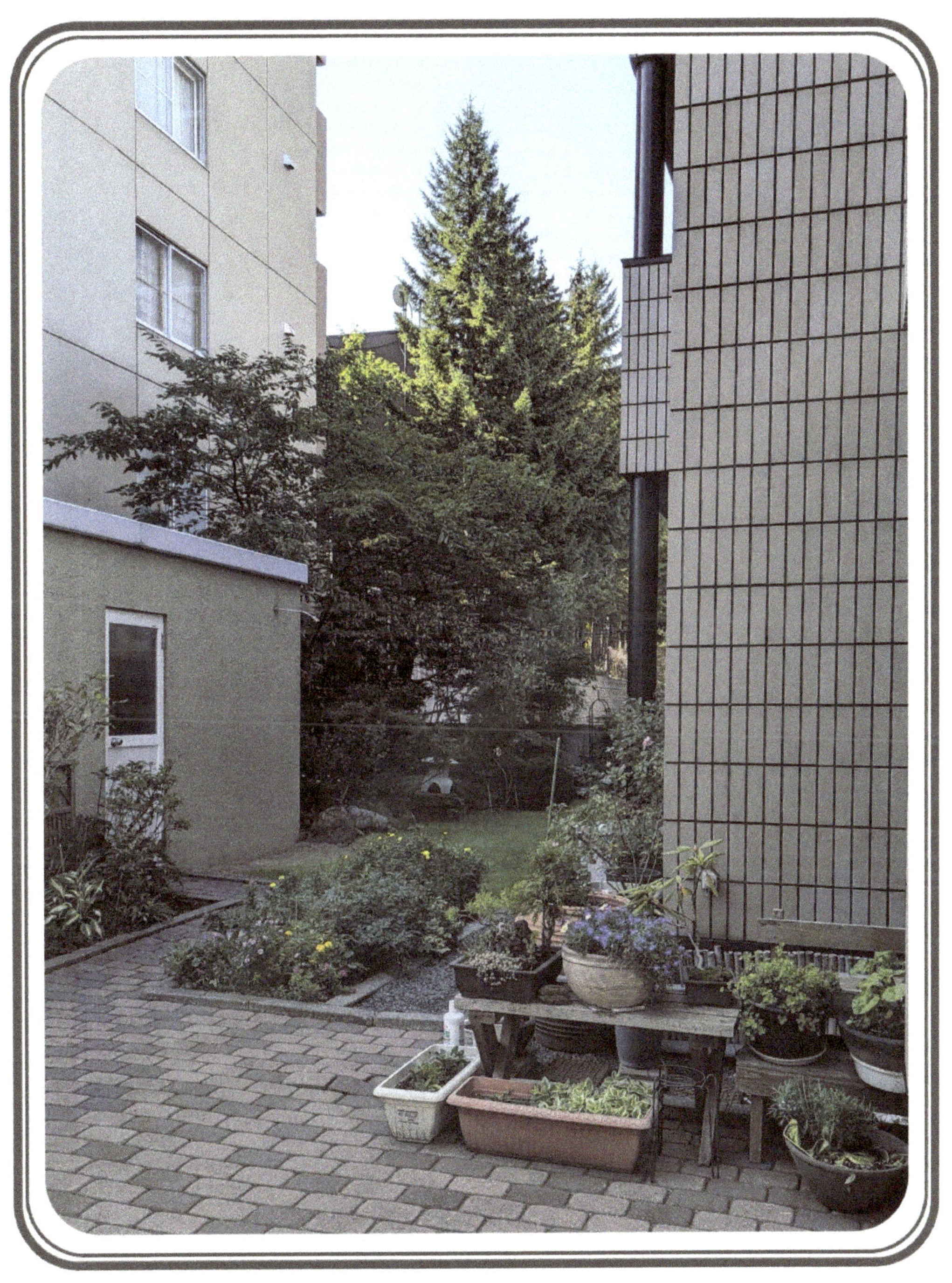

MOTHER

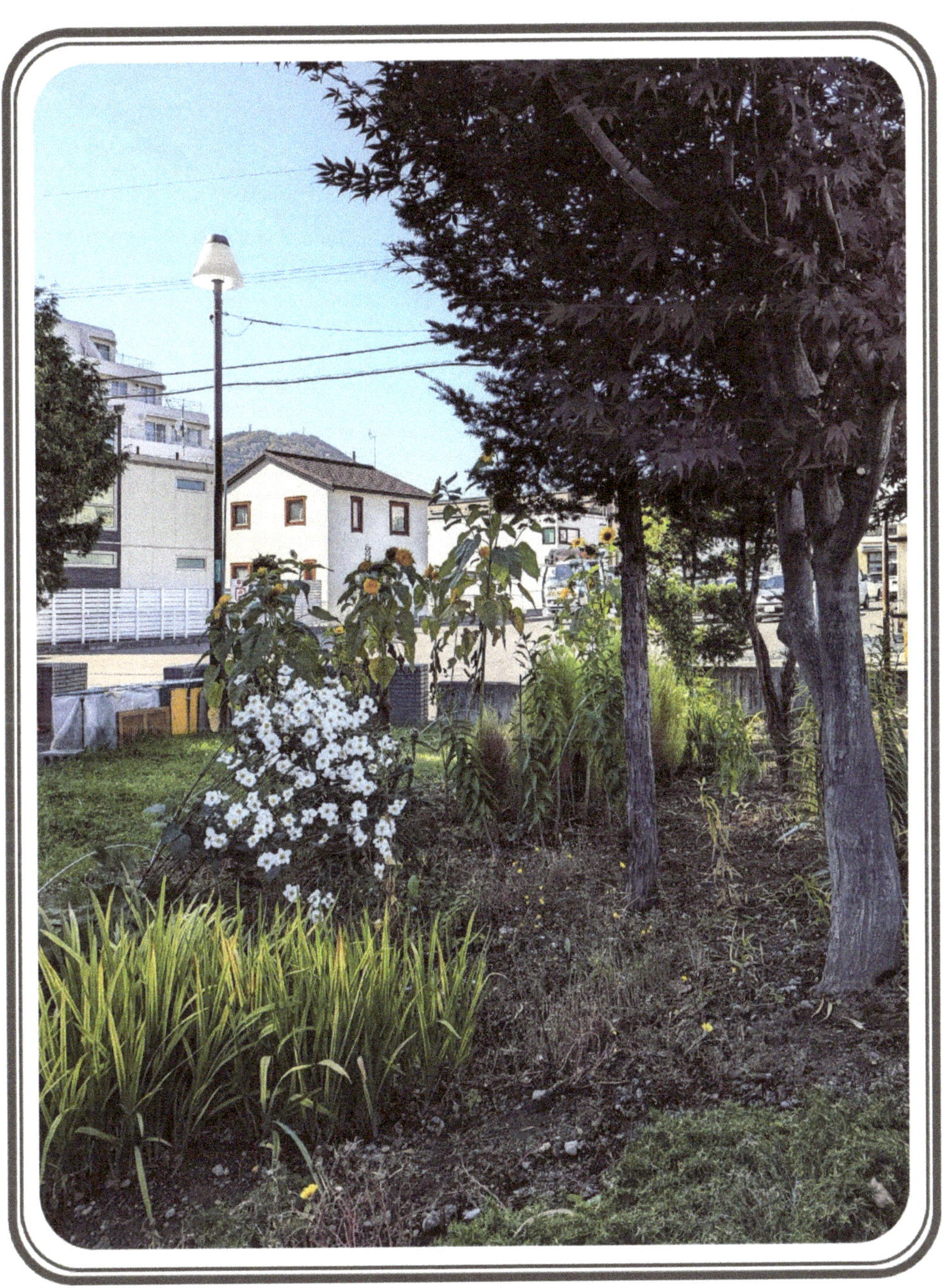

HOOKED

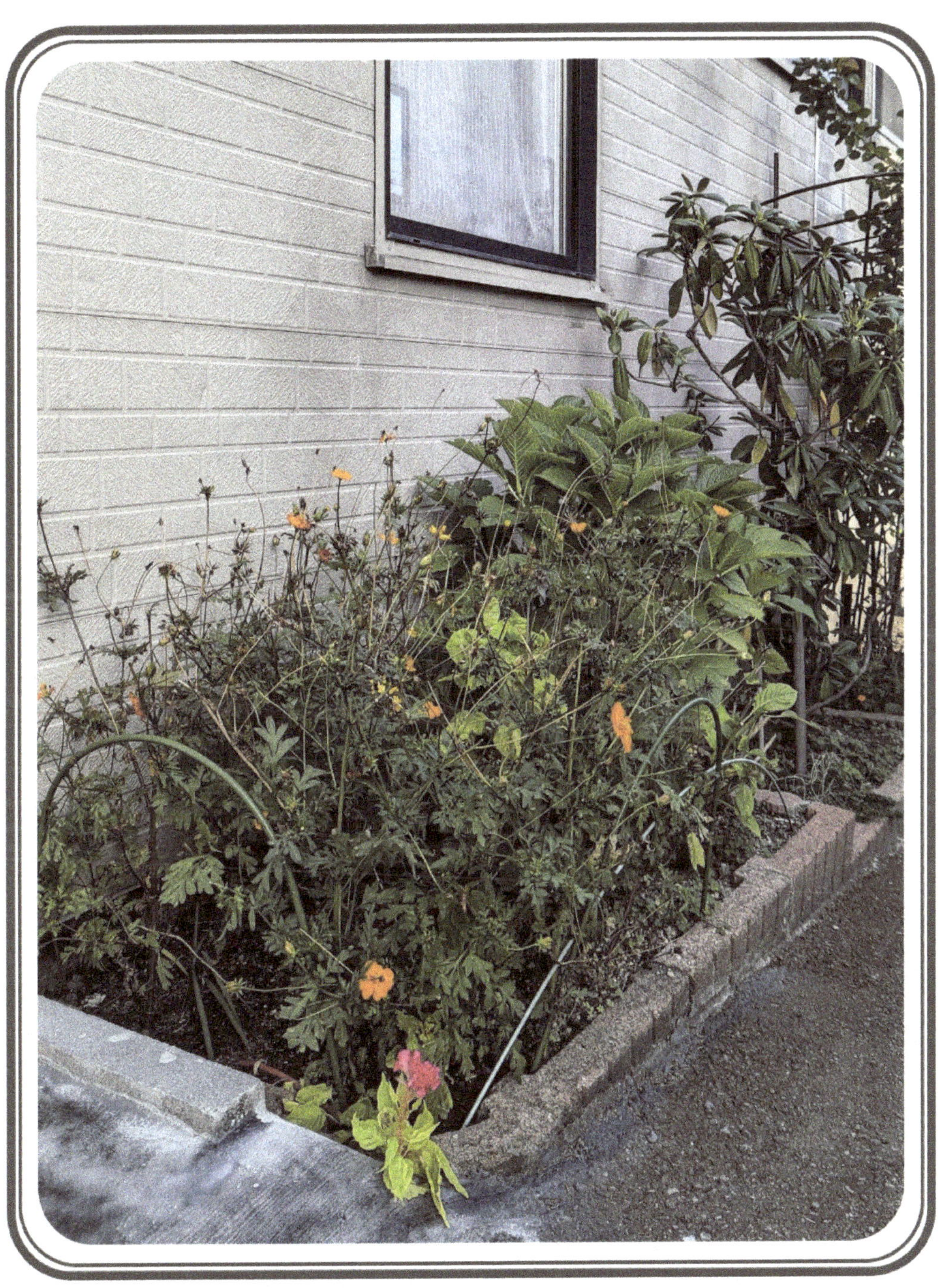

RHUMBA

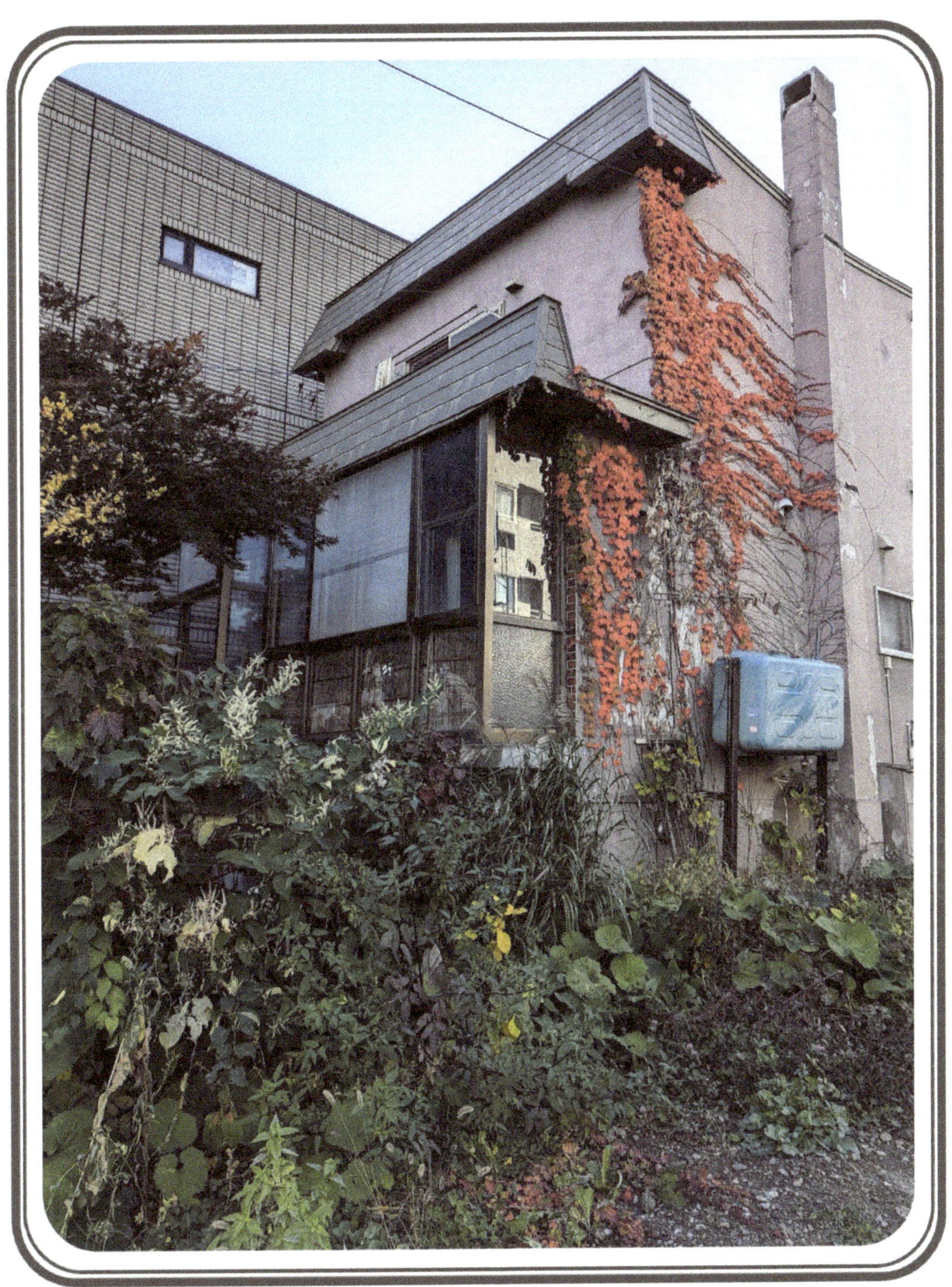

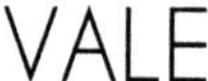

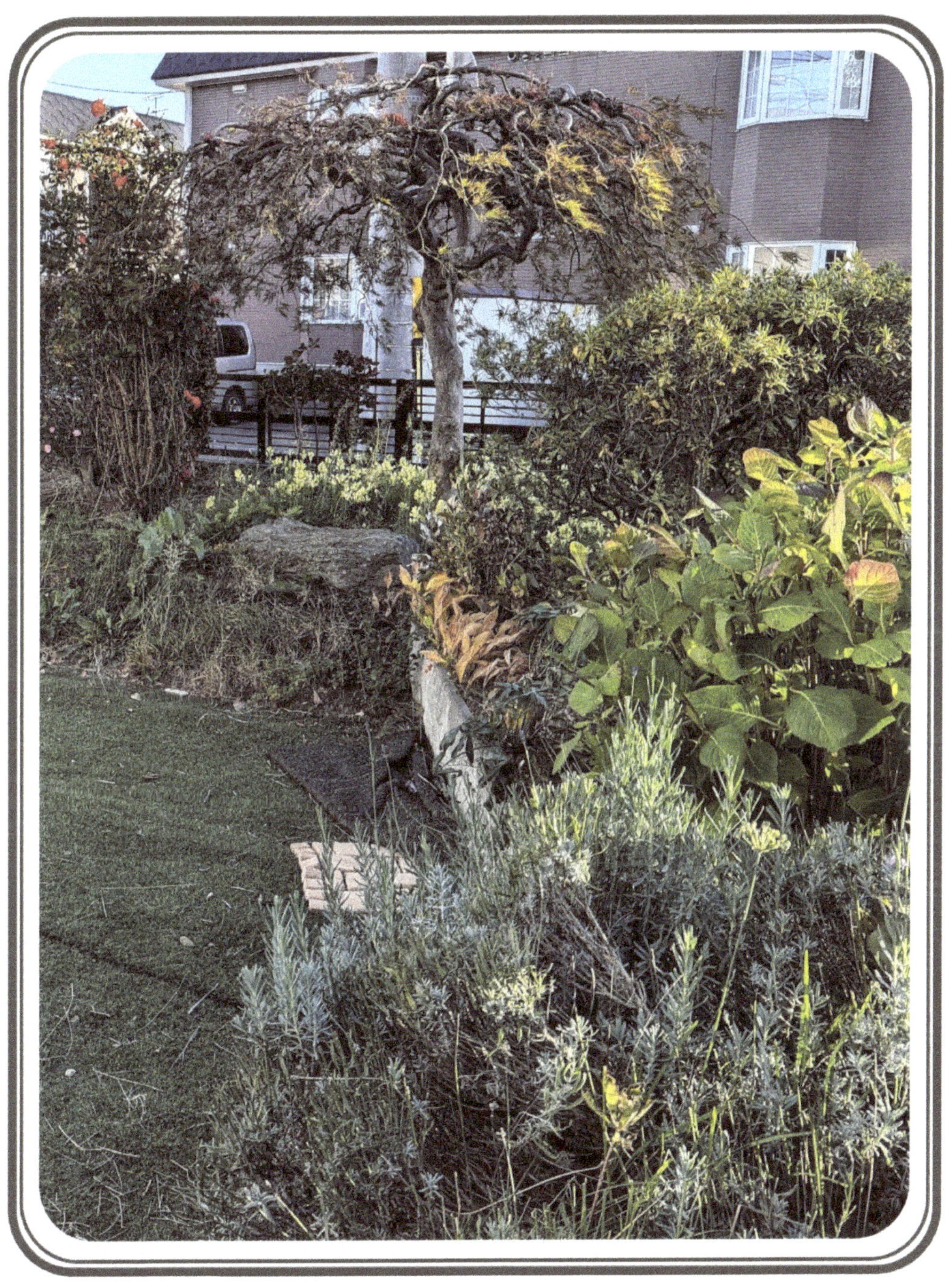

TILLED

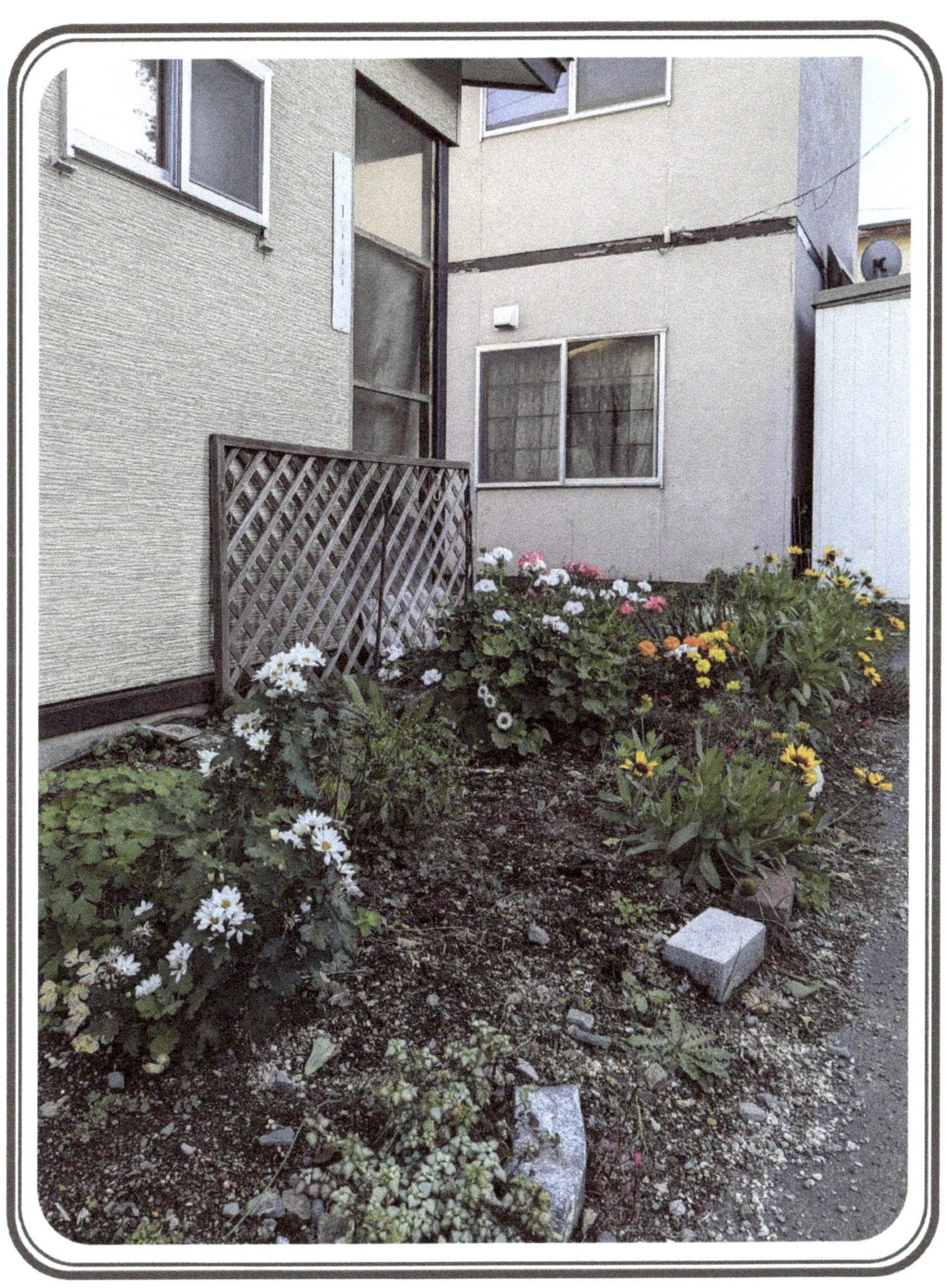

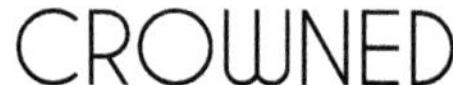
CROWNED

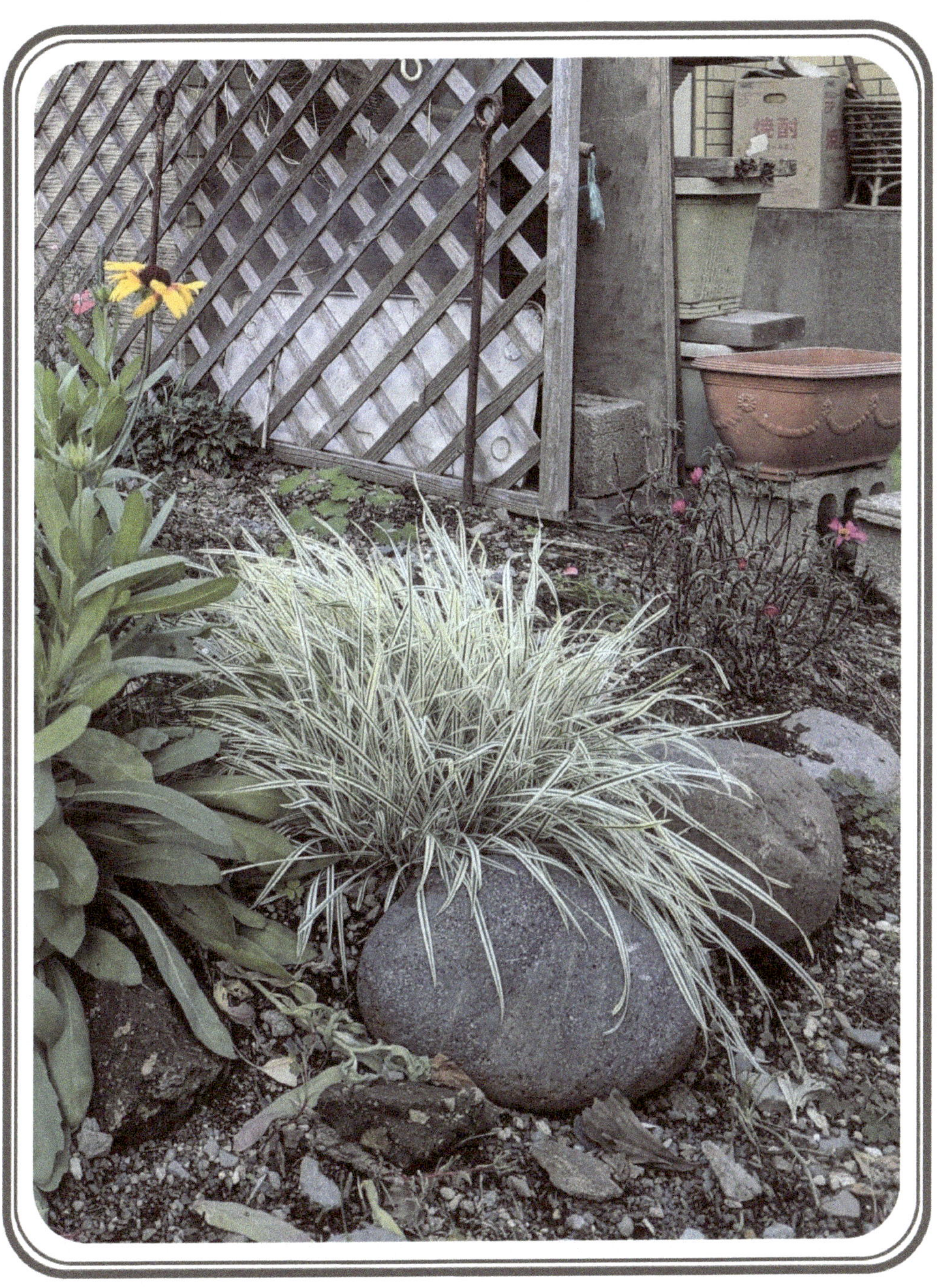
焼酎

THICKET

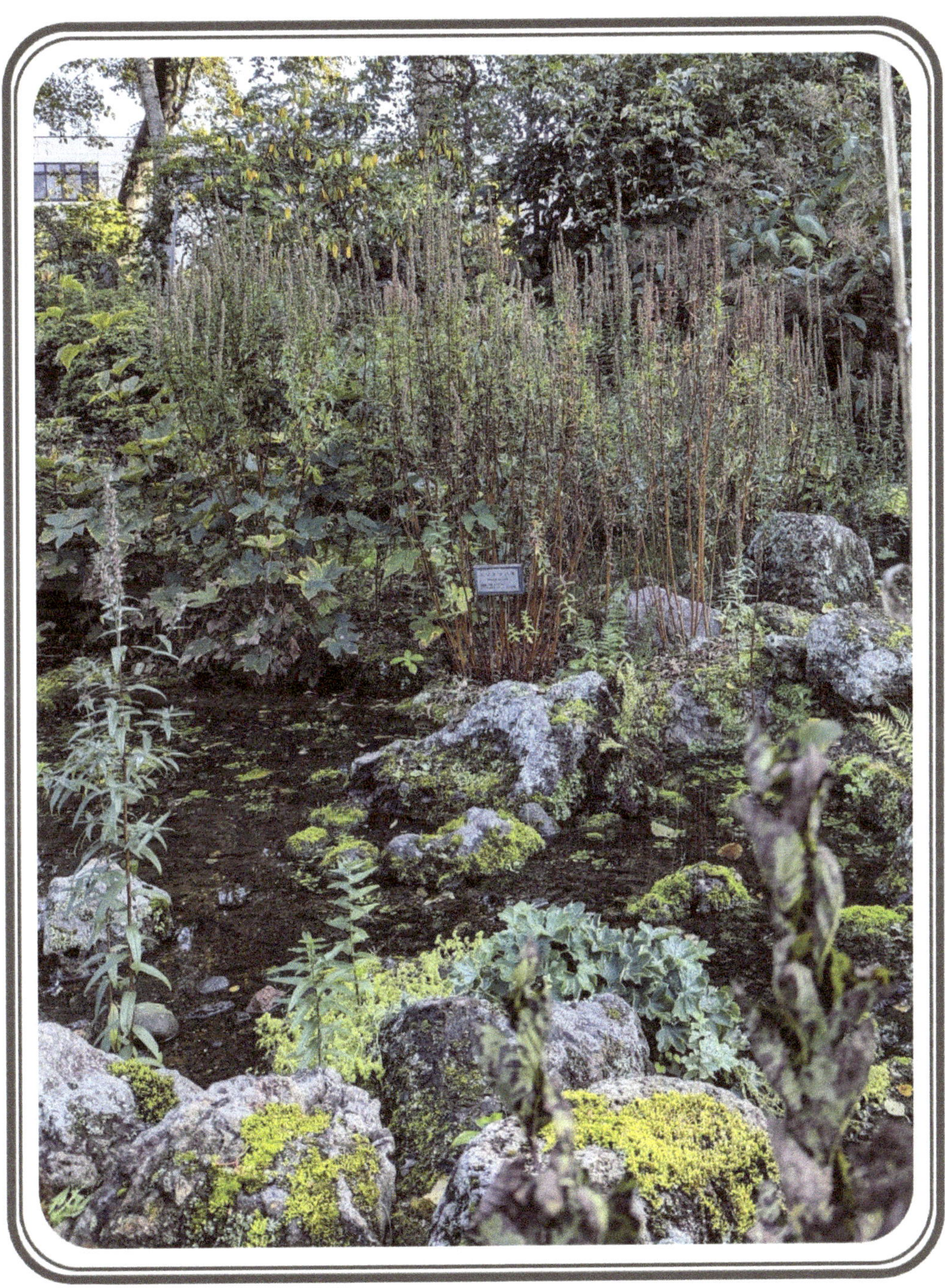

TITLES IN THIS SERIES

Gardens of Sapporo, Japan
Mt. Moiwa, Sapporo, Japan
Shrines of Sapporo, Japan
Parks of Sapporo, Japan
Sapporo City, Japan

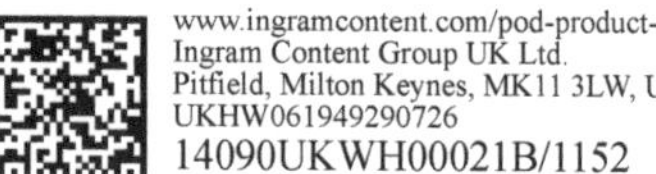

www.ingramcontent.com/pod-product-compliance
Ingram Content Group UK Ltd.
Pitfield, Milton Keynes, MK11 3LW, UK
UKHW061949290726
14090UKWH00021B/1152

9 781951 389321